EXPLORING
THE HILL

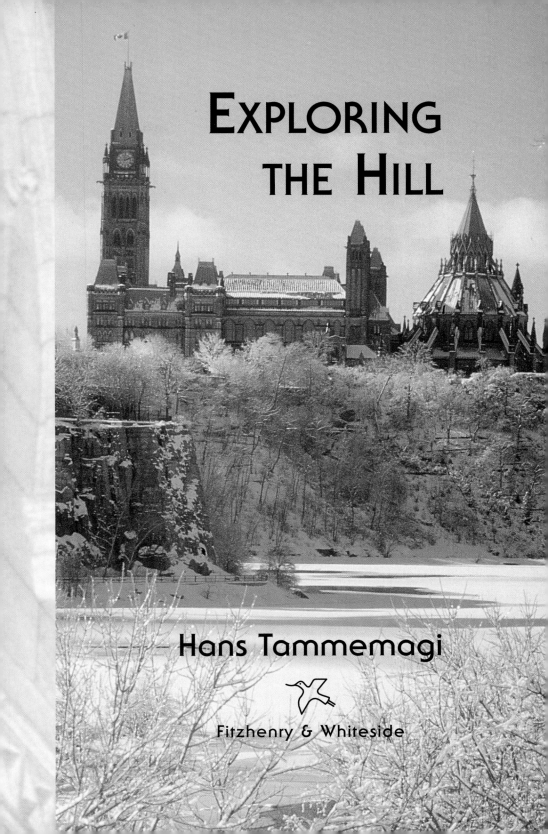

EXPLORING THE HILL

Hans Tammemagi

Fitzhenry & Whiteside

Fitzhenry and Whiteside Limited
195 Allstate Parkway
Markham, Ontario L3R 4T8

In the United States:
121 Harvard Avenue, Suite2
Allston, Massachusetts 02134

www.fitzhenry.ca   godwit@fitzhenry.ca

Fitzhenry & Whiteside acknowledges with thanks the Canada Council for
the Arts, the Government of Canada through its Book Publishing Industry
Development Program, and the Ontario Arts Council for their support of
our publishing program.

National Library Cataloguing-in-Publication Data

Tammemagi, H. Y.

Exploring the Hill : a guide to Canada's Parliament past and
present / Hans Tammemagi.

Includes index.
ISBN 1-55041-641-3

1.Parliament Buildings (Ottawa, Ont.)   I.Title.

NA4415.C22O77   2002   725'.11'0971384   C2002-901611-8

U.S. Cataloging-in-Publication Data

Tammemagi, Hans.
Exploring the hill : a guide to Canada's Parliament past and
present / Hans Tammemagi.— 1st ed.

[152] p. : photos. (some col.), maps ; cm.
Includes index.

Summary: A guide to Canada's Parliament, including new insights into
the original and ongoing planning, construction and design; background on
features such as hidden corridors and secret staircases, and details such as the
magnificent wood and stone carvings, decorative metalwork and plaster
ornamentation.

ISBN 1-55041-641-3 (pbk.)

1. Parliament buildings (Ottawa, Ont.) — History.   2. Canada. Parliament (The
buildings) — History.   3. Public buildings — Ontario — Ottawa.   I. Title.

 971.3 / 84 21   CIP   F1059.5.O9.T36 2002

Cover and interior design: Kinetics Design & Illustration
Cover images courtesy of: National Capital Commission

Printed and bound in Canada
Printed by Goodycolor Inc.

Contents

The Statue of D'Arcy McGee   – HANS TAMMEMAGI

The Heart and Soul
of a Nation

I love wandering around the eccentric, yet elegant old sandstone buildings on Parliament Hill, particularly on a sunny day in the fall after the tourists have gone. Alone without the crush of crowds, you can sense something in the air, you start to feel you are standing in a special place. It is more than the serene dignity of the soaring towers or the majestic vistas. There is a feeling of history, a comprehension that the ground you're walking on is the epicentre from which seismic swells have rolled time and again across this vast nation.

One late afternoon, as the sun slapped broad bands of orange, vermilion and gold against the western horizon, I sat at the foot of D'Arcy McGee's bronze statue that stands behind the soaring shape of the Library. My back rested against a block of granite, polished to a smooth lustre and warm from the sun. *From what part of the rugged Precambrian Shield had this rocky slab been wrenched?* I recalled my geology lessons and imagined it forming from molten lava, cooling and crystallizing thousands of millions of years ago. It waited passively through the eons as the continent around it took shape then uncomplaining, it bore the weight of giant glaciers that ground slowly to and fro, leaving a trail of drumlins, eskers, and moraines scattered across the landscape. As the ice receded, an endless wilderness of lakes and forests emerged. Then, this granite slab felt the soft beat of human footsteps, perhaps witnessed the passing of a canoe, its gunnels high with beaver pelts, or a prospector trudging past laden with bags of ore. And now here it was, a support for McGee, and temporarily for me, a silent witness to the formation and growth of a nation.

McGee, the transplanted Irishman whose eloquence and passion were

1

crucial in persuading the colonies to accept Confederation, towered above me, his face turned toward the Centre Block. Oblivious to the two pigeons perched on his head, McGee's eyes were focussed intently ahead, as though he were trying to envisage the future of the still-new country he helped shape. The sinking sun bathed the buttresses and the old yellow and brown sandstone blocks of the Library in a soft, golden light, their hues changing to gentle pastels. Behind me, far below the hilltop, the waters of the Ottawa River shimmered and danced in the fading light.

I closed my eyes. In the gentle whisper of the breeze I could hear something. Against my back I thought I felt a tremor, just the slightest reverberation as though the granite block was shaking itself from a long slumber. Then I distinguished a voice. It began softly but slowly gained strength until it boomed out, mesmerizing with its rich, Irish lilt. It was McGee. I imagined him as he stood before his fellow parliamentarians, persuading them, compelling them to end their senseless bickering and to forge one powerful, united country. I listened, entranced, as McGee forcefully described what a mighty Dominion could be fashioned; he

Centre Block in fog

– Janet Brooks

2

Sandstone and wrought iron fence with the Peace Tower in background — Hans Tammemagi

Gate, snow and Centre Block — JANET BROOKS

exhorted his colleagues and countrymen to share in and contribute to his vision.

Then I imagined other voices floating on the warm evening breeze. These too were powerful voices, spoken by leaders who shaped this country and guided it through the rocky reefs of history: Sir John A. Macdonald arguing for Confederation in his feisty Scottish brogue, William Lyon Mackenzie King providing firm reassurances through the second great war, John Diefenbaker with his fiery oratory in support of the Prairie farmer, and Pierre Trudeau clinically dissecting those opposed to a new constitution.

The chiming of the carillon bells from high up in the Peace Tower woke me from my reverie. The sun slipped below the horizon and a chill began to settle on the Hill. Only the granite, still retaining the day's warmth, and the very tip of the Peace Tower, where a lonely ray of sunshine glinted, fought a rearguard battle against the descending darkness.

Pulling on a sweater, I slowly walked toward the twinkling lights of Wellington Street, past the West Block, its friendly yellow sandstone blocks now transformed into sombre shades by the dusk.

I love daydreaming with D'Arcy McGee and his bronze companions, for this spot is more than just a hill and a cluster of magnificent build-

4

ings — it is the heart of Canada. This is where our nation's history has been written, and where its hand continues to write. The earliest explorers passed below these cliffs; the Fathers of Confederation met and argued in the chambers of these buildings; the sturdy stone walls have impassively witnessed the evolving affairs of this nation through generations of war and peace. The Hill is Canada, past, present and future. It is both a living museum, and a mighty symbol of our country. There is no better place to learn about this land than here, on this splendid and prominent hilltop.

The buildings, alone, are extraordinary — the finest pile of stones in Canada. When viewed from a distance, they accentuate the cliff on which they are perched, shooting skyward with soaring lines and a complex of towers, chimneys, and a tangle of wrought-iron filigree. William Wilfred Campbell, Canadian poet, felt that the choice of Gothic architecture was most appropriate for the nation's capital because it is "the highest expression of man's aspirations."

The hilltop is also a centre of power, for this is where the nation's laws, the laws affecting us all, are enacted. This is where, through a complex and traditional democratic system, order is enforced on what would otherwise be chaos. It is in these corridors where alliances are brokered and deals are cut, where cabinet ministers are appointed, patronage plums dispensed, and reputations formed and demolished.

There is also a fascinating world that lurks behind-the-scenes of the Hill. The operation of this vast network of people and buildings is no trivial matter. Keeping the machinery of state running smoothly requires a population of about 3,000 people. Not unlike a walled medieval town, the Hill is complete with its own army of services and a tight-knit infrastructure.

Surprisingly, few people know how the Hill actually works and what goes on behind these old walls. The Hill and Parliament are cloaked in traditions whose origins and purposes are buried in the distant past. Let's look behind these veils, then, and explore how this enchanting hilltop intertwines with the history of a nation. You'll see how the buildings emerged from vision to reality out of the midst of wilderness. You'll sit in majestic chambers, peer into nooks and crannies, and climb rickety spiral staircases into lofty towers of what are the best examples of Gothic architecture in North America. You will learn what happens inside the buildings; the arcane and often incomprehensible ways that parliament functions and the ways the laws are created. You'll meet some of the delightful characters who inhabit, and have inhabited, this special spot of Ottawa. And you will also see the modern-day Hill and discover events you can participate in.

So let's begin this journey into the heart of Canada, past and present.

5

The Library, the architectural gem of Canada

Around the Hill

THE three magnificent Gothic buildings with the adjoining Library are the centrepiece of the Hill. They sit on the highest rise of land in Ottawa, some 40 metres above the Ottawa River. Dominating the whole scene is the slender Peace Tower that draws the eyes heavenward.

The soft textures of Nepean sandstone, the primary building stone, contribute to the warmth and charm of these buildings. The blocks of stone have been rough hewn and their coarse finish combine with the always changing hues of yellow, brown, and ochre which give every block a unique character, as though each were an individual work of art framed by its adjoining companions. As you amble along, the walls change in subtle, fascinating ways, all the time adhering to the overall grand theme. What a contrast to modern buildings with their sharp rectangular lines and glassy-smooth finishes.

The buildings have a lightness, almost whimsy, about them, and it is hard to resist a smile as you wander about. There is a madcap lack of symmetry, particularly in the East and West Blocks, as though they care little for the seriously symmetrical, fuddy-duddy Centre Block. While on the Hill, you will be under the ever watchful eye of the face on the tower of the East Block. Is the tower frowning or surprised?

The great empty space that is framed by the three blocks and adorned by the lonely Centennial Flame is often quiet and stark. But it forms a perfect place for national celebrations, such as Canada Day, when it is transformed with tens of thousands of celebrants. It is also a favourite spot for protestors to wave placards, shout slogans, and otherwise exercise the democratic rights so cherished in this country.

But before we describe the Hill and its buildings in detail, let's step back and explore the larger setting in which they are situated.

7

Chapter 2

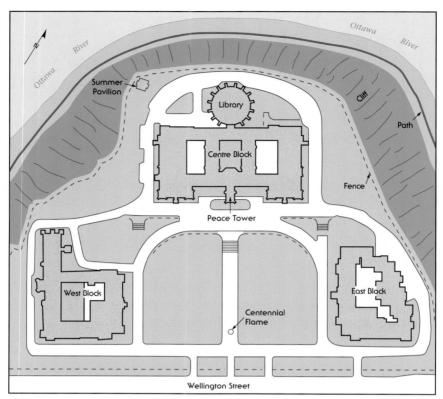

Parliament Hill

Many say that the best place to view the Hill and those magnificent piles of rocks that adorn it are from a distance, where one can gain some sense of how it melds into the surrounding landscape. From Major's Hill Park, on a late afternoon as the sun dips low in the sky, the old stone buildings are transformed into deep blue shadows silhouetted against the golden sky. The Parliament Buildings stand guard alone on this promontory, imperiously aloof, and form a breathtaking vista with the tiny locks of the Rideau Canal at the base of the cliff and the Chaudiere Falls glistening upriver. Across the Ottawa River are Hull and the province of Quebec, with the Gatineau Hills rolling in ever deepening shades of green to the horizon.

The southern side of the Hill offers a distinctly different landscape, for here the land slopes gently toward the skyscrapers and commercial buildings that form downtown Ottawa. Yet the flowing lines of the Parliament Buildings don't clash with their modern surroundings, but instead merge comfortably with the crowded, concrete cityscape.

Wellington Street forms a boundary between the stately grounds of

Aerial view of Hill, 1960   – CITY OF OTTAWA ARCHIVES CA8231

the Hill and the bustle of the crowded downtown core. The street was opened in 1827 as a pedestrian walkway joining Chaudiere and Sappers bridges, with a turnstile at each end to prevent officers' cows from escaping their Barrack's Hill pasture. The area along Wellington Street facing the Hill and to the south of it consists of properties that were acquired by the federal government in the 1960s and 70s. These provide office space for civil servants in what is called the Parliamentary Precinct.

The Hill has profoundly influenced the city that has grown and prospered around it. Drawn by the splendour of the Parliament Buildings, many other prominent edifices, such as the National Library and Archives, the Supreme Court, and the American Embassy have been erected nearby — but none rival those buildings that stand proudly on the highest point of land. Since its earliest days the Hill has always been the central focus of Ottawa.

The Ceremonial Route

The best way to experience this region is to walk or bicycle along the Ceremonial Route, a circle tour that not only offers unsurpassed views of the Hill, but also winds along many other landmarks, such as the National Art Gallery and the Canadian Museum of Civilization. You will travel the same path that visiting dignitaries are shown. If walking, allow at least two hours, and preferably more as there are many fascinating places to explore along the way.

The Ceremonial Route starts in front of the Parliament Buildings,

Around the Hill

proceeds westward along Wellington Street, crosses the Ottawa River to include a stretch in Hull, and then returns via the Alexandra Bridge. Also known as the Confederation Boulevard, the route has been travelled by countless dignitaries and foreign heads of state. And not surprisingly, it not only offers wonderful views of the Hill but also takes you past some of the major cultural and architectural centres of Ottawa. As it forms a circle, you can start anywhere and go in either direction. I have chosen the Centennial Flame as our starting point. We will initially travel west, going clockwise around the loop. Major points of interest that you'll encounter along the way are described below.

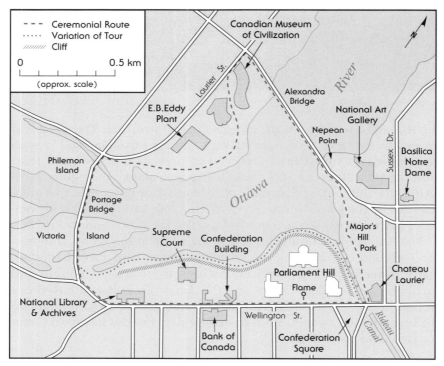

The Ceremonial Route

Directly across Wellington Street is the National Capital Commission information centre, well worth a stop for brochures and other tourist information. To the west is the building previously occupied by the American Embassy before it moved in 2000 to new quarters on Sussex Drive. The prominent position directly across from the Parliament Buildings reflects the close ties between the USA and Canada. The building was constructed in 1932 and was upgraded from a consular office to an embassy in 1943.

The Bank of Montreal at 144 Wellington was constructed in 1931. It is one of the finest examples of Modern Classicism to be found in all the country. Go inside and admire the interior, including a high, slightly-arched ceiling, flags, marble floors, long elegant counters, glorious chandeliers and stone carvings of the coats of arms of the provinces. The exterior is made of limestone taken from the Queenston quarry in Niagara. The main floor and entryway feature beautiful inlaid stonework; the counters are Italian marble breccia. Panels above the windows were carved by New York sculptor Emil Sieben, and depict scenes of Canadian industry and commerce. The Bank of Montreal Building received the Gold Medal from the Royal Architectural Institute of Canada in 1932.

The National Press Club and Press Gallery is located at 150 Wellington Street. It has a membership of over 400 ink-soaked journalists who report the news ever emanating from the Hill.

The Wellington Building, next on the south side of Wellington Street, originally housed the Metropolitan Life Insurance Company. Its cornerstone beside the main entrance displays the date of its construction, November 4, 1925. Today the building forms part of the Parliamentary Precinct containing federal offices. It is closed to the public.

Across the street on the north side are the Confederation building and the old Justice building. They mimic the Parliament Buildings with their yellowish sandstone and distinctive steep roofs. But they are of more modest design, except for the lovely wrought-iron weather vane atop the eastern Confederation Building. The cornerstone was laid in July 1, 1927, and the building was completed in 1930. These are government buildings and are not open to the public. Carved in stone over the western entrance to the western building is the word "Justice," reminiscent of the department it initially housed. The façade is decorated with a few stone carvings, including classic depictions of an Aboriginal warrior and a coureur-de-bois.

The Bank of Canada at 234

Stone carvings on the old Justice building
– HANS TAMMEMAGI

The Supreme Court of Canada   – Phillipe Landreville Inc./Supreme Court of Canada

Wellington Street offers an unusual contrast between yesteryear and today, as the original old stone building has been preserved inside the sleek glass and steel of the new edifice. This site is well worth a visit as there is a Currency Museum as well as an atrium so lush with plants that it looks like an exotic jungle. In the museum you will tread over a veritable fortune, as Canada's gold bullion reserves are stored in the basement below your feet. The gold was stored in the vaults of the East Block until 1938 when it was moved to the present location.

Across the street is the Supreme Court of Canada. The cornerstone was laid on May 19, 1939, by Queen Elizabeth and King George VI, but due to the war, the Supreme Court did not move here until 1946. Initially in 1875 when the Supreme Court was created, it sat in the Railway Committee Room in the Centre Block and then in a stone building on Bank Street, which has since been demolished.

Statues of two ladies, *Veritas* (Truth) and *Justitia* (Justice), flank the stairs to the entrance. Tours are available from 9 to 5 from May 1 to August 31. From September to April, tours must be pre-arranged by calling the Supreme Court or the National Capital Commission. It is rewarding just to pop into the splendid lobby with its high ceiling supported by four large doric columns. As discussed in Chapter 9, the judiciary plays an important role in ensuring a democratic governmental process in Canada. The Supreme Court is the court of final appeal and consists of a chief justice and eight judges, at least three of whom hail from Quebec. Appointed by federal cabinet, the judges serve until the retirement age of 75. The Supreme Court hears cases from the Courts of Appeal of all provinces and territories, as well as federal cases regarding such issues as immigration, taxation, and constitutional matters. One hundred and twenty cases are heard on average each year; these are open to the public.

A stroll behind the building reveals a fountain and a great view of the Hill. From here the Centre Block and Library look like a medieval castle, perched high on a hill with an unobstructed view of the river below.

Across the street is St. Andrews Presbyterian Church, originally built in 1828 by the same stonemasons who constructed the Rideau Canal. It was demolished and reconstructed in 1873. Note how beautifully it has been integrated into the modern office building behind it.

Two government buildings, the East (284 Wellington Street) and West Memorial buildings are on the south side of Wellington, one on each side of Lyon Street. The two blocks are mirror images of each other and are joined by an elevated walkway, which carries inscriptions commemorating those that fell during the Second World War. These buildings, housing the Justice Department (east) and National Archives (west), are not open to the public.

The National Library and the National Archives of Canada share the same building on the north side of Wellington Street. The National Library, which is responsible for collecting and preserving Canada's published heritage, stores 18 million volumes on 160 kilometres of steel shelving. The National Archives stores the memory of Canada on millions of films, maps, diaries, treaties, journals, photographs, sound recordings and much more. Both organizations regularly present fascinating displays and seminars.

Turn right and cross Portage Bridge. Victoria Island is worth a brief stop with its abandoned old stone building and lonely chimney, a remnant of the Ottawa Carbide Company Mill, operated by Thomas Leopold "Carbide" Willson (1816–1915), a prolific inventor in the fields of electricity, metallurgy, fertilizers, and electrochemistry. He won international fame in 1892 for developing calcium carbide from which acetylene is produced. Acetylene was used for illumination and to manufacture industrial hydrochemicals. Victoria Island is the subject of a Native land claim and for some years has been occupied in protest by a group of Aboriginals. At the east end is a wooden stockade which houses the Aboriginal Experience highlighting the culture and tradition of the First Nations. Included are a trading post, guided tours, Native foods, and dancers. The eastern end of the island offers excellent views of Parliament Hill.

Next, continue northward and cross Philemon Island. Take a moment to pause on the bridge and note the lumber factory to the west, a small remnant of the once-burgeoning industry that helped create Hull and

Ottawa. The views to the east are grand and include the Parliament Buildings and the National Art Gallery. Portage Bridge itself is of historic note as it was constructed in 1828, linking the two relatively isolated villages. Turn right onto Voyageur Pathway as soon as you are off the bridge. This part of the tour offers lovely views of the Hill; note how the West Block looks disdainfully isolated from the Centre Block. Next you will

A painting of Parliament Hill as seen from Major's Hill Park, 1882
– CITY OF OTTAWA ARCHIVES CA 4232

pass the E. B. Eddy paper factory on your left, once a dominant employer in the region.

Rounding the corner you'll find the distinct modern curves of the Canadian Museum of Civilization. Shunning the rectilinear lines of its neighbours, the terraced Museum seems to melt into the landscape. Even the grounds form part of the museum, with totem poles, an airplane, and other exhibits. Go up the broad stairs between the two museum buildings and, if you have never visited the museum before, take the time to pop in and view the stunning main feature — dozens of colourful, full-size West Coast totem poles (these can be viewed for free from the main lobby). Completed in 1989, the museum has three floors of exhibits spanning the entire scope of human life, with special emphasis on Canada. It also holds a Children's Museum and an IMAX theatre.

Proceed along Laurier Street and turn right onto Alexandra Bridge, built in 1900. The bridge's wooden decking rattles pleasantly as the wheels of cars and bicycles pass over. It's sure to feel comfortable under your tired feet. When you reach the south side of the river, cross to the east side of the street and visit the National Art Gallery. Built in 1988, this wonderful glass fairy cake is an architectural gem with subtle parallels to the Parliament Buildings across the river. The glass design is light and airy and beckons you to enter and enjoy the 2,000 works of art that are on display. There is no better place for lunch than in the cafeteria, surrounded by internationally acclaimed paintings, sculptures, and panoramic views of the sparkling Ottawa River and the Hill beyond it.

Behind the Art Gallery on the river side is Nepean Point. This piece of land contains a monument to Samuel de Champlain who first passed this way in 1613. The monument was unveiled in 1915, and the open-air theatre, Astrolabe Theatre, opened in 1967.

Cross back to the west side of the street. Up ahead and to the left you will see the twin spires of Notre Dame Basilica, the oldest surviving church in Ottawa. Construction began in 1841 and was complete by 1865. Next you will enter Major's Hill park, a gem that offers some of the best views of the Hill anywhere. When Colonel By built his residence on the eastern cliff, the promontory became known as Colonel's Hill. When Major Bolton succeeded By as chief of the town's garrison in 1832, the name changed to Major's Hill. In 1866, Major's Hill became Ottawa's first public park. For several years, Major's Hill was slated as the building site of the Governor General's residence, but financial difficulties encountered in constructing the Parliament Buildings led to the more economical residence of Rideau Hall southeast of the Hill. The park features excellent views of Parliament Hill and the locks of the Rideau Canal as well as a statue of Colonel John By, the British officer who built the 200-kilometre-long Rideau Canal and founded Bytown, now Ottawa.

Proceed in a southerly direction keeping to the right (west) side of the Chateau Laurier hotel. This imposing building was built in 1912 of granite, limestone, and capped with copper. Next door is Union Station (now the Conference Centre), which was constructed by the Grand Trunk Railway in the same year. Also take in the Rideau Canal, an engineering achievement that moulded the early history of Ottawa, and today plays a significant role in defining its urban character. These eight locks lift boats 24 metres from the river to the first long stretch of canal that extends through the city. Note the craftsmanship; made of Ottawa limestone, these locks are still intact and functional after more than 170 years of use.

On the right-hand side just before the canal bridge is the Canadian Museum of Contemporary Photography, well worth a visit. It houses more than 160,000 photographs from some of Canada's most dynamic photographers. Now head west crossing the bridge called Connaught Plaza. It originally consisted of two bridges: Sappers Bridge on the south side (built in 1827) and Dufferin Bridge (built in 1872).

Down the slope to the right are two stone buildings situated on the west side of the canal. The first is the original lock master's house; the second is the Bytown Museum, the oldest existing building in Ottawa. It was built by Colonel By in 1827 and was called the Commissariat Building, a three-storey warehouse that originally stored Rideau Canal building supplies.

Return to Wellington Street and continue westward. On the left you will see Confederation Square, begun in 1927 at the confluence of Ottawa's oldest streets: Wellington, Elgin, and Rideau. The centrepiece of the square is the War Memorial, unveiled in 1939 by King George VI.

Commanding the southwest corner of Wellington and Elgin Streets is the Langevin Block, the most distinctive and historic building in the Parliamentary Precinct. Built between 1883 and 1889 directly across from the East Block, and originally known as the South Block, it was the first major federal building constructed after the Parliament Buildings. It was constructed to house the fast-expanding civil service, which had already outgrown the East and West Blocks. Designed by Thomas Fuller, the architect of Centre Block, Langevin Block combines elements of Italian Renaissance Revival and French Second Empire periods. Four stories high with a green, copper, steep-sloping roof, it is a fine complement to the Parliament Buildings. Yet the Langevin Block, with its monochrome sandstone exterior, and hemmed in by office buildings of a more modern era, has an almost sad, left-out-of-the-party look about it.

The Langevin Building is named after Sir Hector Langevin, one of the Fathers of Confederation and Secretary of State and Superintendent of Indian Affairs under John A. Macdonald. He was probably the most influential Quebecer of his day. The building underwent major renovations in 1974, including the installation of air-conditioning, wall partitions, and false ceilings. The impressive entrance hall with its graceful staircase flanked by polished granite columns was preserved. Langevin Block, rather than Centre Block, should be considered the real centre of power in Canada. Since 1972, it has housed the Prime Minister's Office as well as the Privy Council (i.e., the Cabinet). Unfortunately, it is not open to the public.

Now you are back at Centennial Flame and the magnificent Parliament Buildings. The Ceremonial Route is complete.

A Variation on the Ceremonial Route

For those interested in a more nature-oriented outing, we offer this variation on the Ceremonial Route. Start at Centennial Flame and go east along the north side of Wellington Street. Just before the Rideau Canal turn left and descend past the Bytown Museum to the Ottawa River. Bear left and proceed west along the river on the pathway located at the base of the Hill. This tour is much the same as the Ceremonial Route but you don't visit the buildings along Wellington, although you will see the rears of those on the north side of the street. The route follows a serene, quiet path that lies in the shadow of the formidable cliff. Along the base of this escarpment you'll come across various alder, oak and sugar maples. It is not uncommon to spot songbirds in the trees and on the river, Canada Geese, ringbilled gulls and a variety of ducks. If you're lucky, you might also catch a glimpse of a racoon or two, perhaps even a red fox. The path you'll follow is paved and has frequent park benches as well as good lighting at night. It forms part of the 170-kilometre-long Capital Pathway, one of the most extensive recreational pathways in North America. You can look up the thickly wooded cliff or across the waters at the province of Quebec and the City of Hull. The Parliament Buildings are shielded by the thickly wooded cliffs, but as the path curves into an embayment you are rewarded by a good view of the Confederation Building and the Supreme Court. A short distance westward is the Cliff Street central heating plant, which provides the steam and chilled water that heats and cools Parliament Hill and many other federal buildings in the Parliamentary Precinct. When you reach Portage Bridge, turn right, and proceed as on the Ceremonial Route.

If you are interested in further exploration near and beyond the Parliament Buildings, the Mile of History is recommended. This route passes along Sussex Drive past the prime minister's home to Rideau Hall and includes the War Museum, the Mint, and the colourful Byward Market. Most Ottawa guide books will provide further details.

Around the Hill

Parliament Hill in the fall

The Birth
of a Nation

TRACES of Native camps dating back 5,000 years have been exhumed along the banks of the Ottawa River. More recently, Algonquin inhabited western Quebec and eastern Ontario including the site of today's Parliament Hill. The Algonquin were hunters living in bands of related families. They controlled the Ottawa River and its tributaries, the main travel route in eastern Canada, and served an important function as traders facilitating commerce between neighbouring peoples. The area around present-day Ottawa, located at the confluence of three rivers — the Ottawa, Rideau, and Gatineau — formed a natural meeting place. The word "Ottawa" comes from the Algonquian "Odawa" meaning "to trade." The relationship between the Algonquin and the powerful Iroquois to the south often degenerated into warfare that continued well after European contact.

Samuel de Champlain was one of the first Europeans to see what is now Parliament Hill when he paddled his canoe past the escarpment in June of 1613. The great explorer probably spared no more than a passing glance at the heavily wooded promontory that rises high above the river. Instead, Champlain's attention was focused on traversing the foaming, swirling waters of the rapids he named *La Chaudière*, the cauldron. Over the next 150 years, other explorers, including Brulé, Radisson, LaVérendrye, Mackenzie, and Thompson sweated their way up the Ottawa en route to the interior of North America. But no heed was paid to the Hill.

The French established a comprehensive fur trade along the Ottawa River which formed part of the main transportation route into the wilderness. For almost two centuries the Hill saw no permanent settlers, only canoes heading upriver with coureurs-de-bois beating against the current and returning, their boats laden with the pelts of beaver, muskrat, and mink.

The lumber trade began in the early 1800s and giant pines were felled by the thousands every winter and were floated down river every spring.

Log boom below the Hill   – CITY OF OTTAWA ARCHIVES CA0158

The Hill sat silent witness to the giant log rafts that thundered over Chaudière Falls, and to the rise of the rough-and-tumble lumber camp called Wright's Town (later renamed Hull). The seemingly endless stands of virgin pine were like gold mines that helped transform some of the more ambitious into lumber barons and gave steady employment to thousands.

In 1802, a 240-hectare block of land that included present-day Parliament Hill was granted to Jacob Carman, the son of a United Empire Loyalist. Ten years later, the Hill and surrounding land were purchased by Thomas Fraser for twelve pound Nova Scotia currency. It turned out the land, though offering wonderful vistas of the Ottawa River and surrounding landscape, was not well suited for farming or for logging.

In 1823, Governor Lord Dalhousie, acting on behalf of the British government, bought it from Fraser's son Hugh for the grand sum of 750 pound sterling. Dalhousie's aim was to build a fort on the strategic site to help protect the northern entrance of the soon-to-be-built Rideau Canal. At the time, American guns commanded a narrow section of the St. Lawrence River at Fort Ogdensburgh. The British, with lingering memories of the War of 1812, decided to build a safer, although longer, passage between Montreal and Kingston.

When Colonel By began construction of the Rideau Canal in 1826, the Royal Miners and Sappers (or what today we call the Army Corps of Engineers), were housed in three wooden, sixteen-room barracks situated on what is now the eastern part of the Centre Block. An officers' quarters was located where the Library now stands. A large stone hospital, which also housed the Miners and Sappers, stood at the north end of the present West Block. The compound was surrounded by a four-metre-high stockade of cedar posts. The site became known as Barracks Hill and the city that was growing rapidly around it, Bytown. From its earliest days, Barracks Hill became the place to hold festive events, such as military parades, open-air concerts, and fireworks on Queen Victoria's birthday — traditions that continue to this day.

The Rideau Canal was completed in 1832 and the inaugural voyage was made by the steamboat *Pumper*. With no more need for the Sappers, the garrison left in 1856 for the Crimean War. The barracks were torn down and the Hill became the location of the town's fall agricultural fair.

The canal and the booming lumber industry brought prosperity. Bytown grew rapidly and was incorporated as the City of Ottawa on January 1, 1855. By 1900, the population of Ottawa reached 60,000. Today, the metropolitan area of Ottawa exceeds 1 million.

The Making of a Country

The history of the Hill and the Canadian parliamentary system is rooted in the years well before Confederation. Let's pick up the story in the early 1800s when the territory that was to become Canada was still a British colony. The French defeat began on the Plains of Abraham in 1759, and four years later Canada was irrevocably ceded to Great Britain with the signing of the Peace of Paris. With the victory, Britain became the dominant force in a territory that included the six colonies: Lower Canada (Quebec), Upper Canada (Ontario), Nova Scotia, New Brunswick, Newfoundland, and Prince Edward Island, as well as Rupert's Land in the north and the large western part of the continent beyond Ontario.

The original British North American colonies were governed in a relatively consistent manner. Each had a governor, who was appointed by the British king or queen and usually served for a term that lasted only a few years. In addition, there was an executive council and a legislative assembly to advise the governor. The executive council could remain in office for decades and in many respects wielded the real power. These executive councils often became oligarchies controlled by a handful of families whose power persisted over generations. Such families became colonial aristocrats and granted themselves powerful positions and large tracts of land.

To the south, the thirteen colonies along the eastern seaboard were becoming increasingly discontent over issues such as trade, taxation, and self-government. In 1776, they declared independence and fought the Revolutionary War with Great Britain to form an autonomous country, the United States of America. Their attempts to capture Quebec and Nova Scotia were thwarted. The boundary between the USA and the British colonies to the north was established in the Treaty of 1783, and although the Americans did their best to revise that boundary in the War of 1812, it has endured. The War of 1812 brought to an end over two

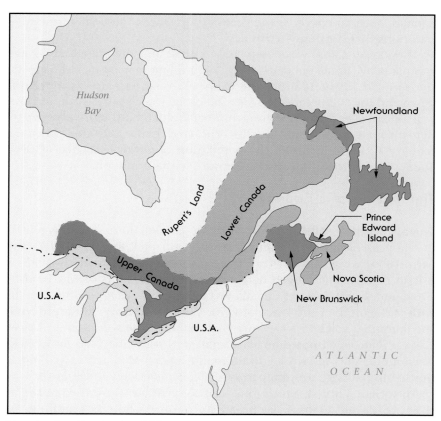

Map of eastern Canada, circa 1838

centuries of territorial conflict and ushered in a peace that has lasted between Canada and the United States to this day.

In Upper Canada (now Ontario), the executive council was known as the Family Compact. For several decades the members of this elite group effectively controlled the colony and its commerce. Eventually, they aroused the collective enmity of farmers, tradesmen, and other ordinary people who, led by William Lyon Mackenzie, demanded representative government. In Lower Canada (Quebec), there were similar political problems and, in addition, there was conflict between French-speaking inhabitants and the English elite. Lower-Canadian opposition to the entrenched ruling class was spearheaded by Louis Joseph Papineau. In 1837, rebellion broke out in both colonies. Although they were quickly suppressed, the revolts forced the British to make changes.

To resolve the issues that fuelled the rebellions, the ruling British instituted "responsible government." This meant that the governor of each colony would have to follow the advice of the executive council, whose members would be part of and responsible to the assembly, which was to be elected by the people.

In addition, Upper and Lower Canada were united into the single colony of Canada in 1840. The capital, originally Kingston, was moved to Montreal in 1843. In 1848, reform governments were elected in both Nova Scotia and Canada that abolished the Family Compacts as well as the veto power of British governors.

In spite of the introduction of responsible government, the union of Upper and Lower Canada was not a happy one. In 1849, the Montreal legislative site was burned to the ground by a pro-British mob. For the next ten years, the Province of Canada had no permanent home for its parliament, which alternated every two years between Toronto and Quebec City, with the attendant massive administrative complications of moving all the files, records and parliamentarians and their staff each time.

To overcome the friction between English and French speakers, the legislation asked Queen Victoria to intervene in choosing a permanent capital. Five cities submitted bids for the honour: Montreal, Toronto, Quebec, Kingston and, to everyone's surprise, Ottawa. Governor General Sir Edmund Head confidentially advised the Queen that the roaring lumber town on the border of the two Canadas might be the "least objectionable choice" as "every city is jealous of every other except Ottawa." Thus Ottawa would win "second vote of every place."

In 1857, Queen Victoria initiated the Canadian tradition of compromise by selecting Ottawa as permanent capital of the colony of Canada. It was rumoured that the Queen had made the choice by playing "pin the tail on the donkey" with a map of British North America. Another story has it that the member of parliament for Ottawa took Lord Edmund

Queen Victoria's statue on Parliament Hill   – HANS TAMMEMAGI

Head, the visiting governor general and the principal advisor to the Queen, to a lavish luncheon on Major's Hill knowing that Lady Head, an amateur artist, would be enthralled by the picturesque site and would make a sketch. All went according to plan, and the drawing was subsequently shown to the Queen, which influenced her final decision.

Queen Victoria's choice, nevertheless, was still controversial as the burgeoning Ottawa was little more than a rough frontier settlement consisting of lumber mills, saloons, and sheds, isolated in the wilderness and far from the comforts of civilization. In fact, it was described by a prominent visitor as a "sub arctic lumber village transformed by royal mandate into a political cockpit." One reason for Ottawa's selection was to ensure that the capital would be a safe distance from its sometimes hostile, southerly neighbour. An American newspaper was quick to point out that in this regard, Ottawa was an excellent choice, "because invading soldiers would get lost looking for it in the bush." Even Governor General Lord Monck remarked, "It seems like an act of insanity to have fixed the Capital of this great country away from the civilization, intelligence, and commercial enterprise of this province, in a place that can never be of importance and where the political section of the community will live in isolation and removed from the action of any public opinion."

Lady Monck, wife of the governor general, wrote in her diary on October 5, 1864, shortly after arriving in Ottawa: "We were much disgusted with the squalid look of Ottawa, though we only saw it by lamplight, which was scarcely any light, such wretched gas. The streets were so rough, like dirt roads. I went on wondering how we ever could live there.... We all groaned over Ottawa; it looks as if it was at 'tother end of nowhere!"

Despite the fuss, construction began on the Parliament Buildings in the early 1860s, and by 1866, they were complete. But Parliament Hill was not to serve the *colony* of Canada for long.

In 1861, the onslaught of the American Civil War threatened the British colonies north of the border. A heavily armed America emerged from the conflict that was expansionist in spirit and bore no love for Britain. It seemed inevitable that America would quickly swallow the lightly armed British colonies to the north. To counter both this armed and economic threat, the Fathers of Confederation persuaded three colonies (Nova Scotia, New Brunswick, and Canada) to join together in 1867 to form the Dominion of Canada.

Confederation, which encompassed concepts from Britain's parliamentary system and elements from the American system, was realized with the passing of the British North America Act by British parliament in March of 1867.

The Birth of a Nation

Sir John A. Macdonald, one of the Fathers of Confederation and Canada's first prime minister
– National Archives of Canada C21290

The former colony of Canada was split into two provinces, Quebec and Ontario. Ottawa, with its magnificent, recently-completed legislative buildings, was selected as the capital of the new nation. This completed the remarkable evolution of Ottawa, from wilderness to rough-and-tumble lumber town, to capital of one of the largest countries in the world. The new Parliament Buildings held only one session of colonial parliament before they became the seat of power for a nation.

Canada was to grow rapidly after this. A powerful new means of transportation, the railway, was just beginning to prove its enormous potential. It would play a key role throughout Canada's early expansion. Rupert's Land and the Northwest Territories became part of Canada in 1870. Manitoba, British Columbia, and Prince Edward Island would join in 1870, 1871, and 1873, respectively.

In 1905, a large part of the Northwest became the provinces of Alberta and Saskatchewan. Finally, in 1949, Newfoundland joined the Dominion. In 1982, the British North America Act was patriated, and, renamed the Constitution Act, which finally made Canada a fully sovereign nation. The last part of the puzzle came with the birth of Nunavut, which emerged from the Northwest Territories in 1999 as a territory of its own.

The First Dominion Day

Festivities in Ottawa marking the birth of the nation were stupendous. At five minutes past midnight on July 1, 1867, a 101-gun salute and the ringing of all the bells in Ottawa marked the moment which initiated a huge party on the Hill which included bonfires and fireworks. The next morning, military bands marched and played as the governor general bestowed honours on the Fathers of Confederation, including a knighthood for Prime Minister John A. Macdonald. Houses throughout town were decorated with flags and banners. Celebrations carried on until evening when everyone poured back to the Hill for more bonfires and fireworks. The happy tradition of fireworks and parties on July 1 has continued to this day, and is particularly well celebrated on the Hill.

Parliament Buildings illuminated for the visit of the Duke of York, 1901.
– NATIONAL ARCHIVES OF CANADA PA030246

The Birth of a Nation

The original Centre Block

Canada's First Parliament Buildings

ON May 7, 1859, an advertisement appeared in Quebec and Ontario newspapers inviting architects to submit designs for public buildings in Ottawa of a "plain, substantial" style. A prize of 250 pounds was offered for the design of the main building with another 250 pounds for design of two departmental buildings. It is amazing that such soaring magnificent buildings were to arise from this simple advertisement — and in the middle of a wilderness. Although the most remarkable and enduring buildings in Canada would eventually emerge, it was not without considerable pain and difficulty.

Three buildings were planned. The central one, Centre Block, was to hold the seats of power, both the House of Commons and the Senate. The two flanking buildings were first known as the Departmental Buildings and were to contain the entire civil service of the colony of Canada.

The making of the Parliament Buildings was undertaken with astonishing — almost reckless — haste. A scant four months after the invitation was issued, the winners were announced.

A total of 32 designs were submitted covering the spectrum of architectural possibilities, from Classic to Italian to Plain Modern. A few of the competitors were accomplished architects; others were to go on to distinguished careers. The winners, Thomas Fuller and Chilion Jones (Centre Block), and Thomas Stent and Augustus Laver (East and West Blocks) had completed no previous works approaching the scale of their proposals. Stent and Laver later had the honour of designing new government buildings in Sydney, Australia. Laver and Fuller went on to design and build the New York state capital at Albany.

The architects selected the soaring Gothic style because it reflected not

Chapter 4

Stone unicorn at the entrance to the Centre Block

– HANS TAMMEMAGI

Thomas Fuller, Dominion Architect

Thomas Fuller was chief architect for the Department of Public Works, effectively the Dominion Architect, from 1881 to 1896. He was responsible for designing federal buildings right across the nation at a critical time when a network of post offices, armouries, and other government buildings was just being established. Fuller helped develop a distinctively Canadian federal style which was modelled, at least in part, on the Centre Block. He was also responsible for designing the Library and the Langevin Building.

Gothic Revival Primer

Gothic revival, also known as Victorian Gothic, is based on the medieval architecture of England and Europe. It is characterized by warmth of colour, soaring towers, flying buttresses, vaulted roofs, pointed arches, and a celebration of ornamentation. It is a creative style that allows freedom of expression, including whimsy, and abhors uniform, rigid geometry and symmetry. It also has a sense of humour.

Gothic was popular in Britain during the mid 1800s and was thought by some to embody the genius of the "British race." With the exception of the British parliament at Westminster, Gothic was a rare architectural style for civil use and was usually seen in churches and educational institutions.

Stone carvings are an appealing and ubiquitous characteristic of Gothic architecture: these are organic and humanistic and include flowers, plants, birds, animals, people as well as mythical creatures such as unicorns, griffons, gargoyles, and grotesques. They are entwined in sinuous patterns based on natural shapes with the figures often distorted or exaggerated.

only the roots of parliamentary democracy developed from the Middle Ages, but also the aspirations of a developing nation. They also felt the Gothic style would provide breathtaking views from two very different perspectives of Parliament Hill: the dramatic cliff top as seen from the river below, and the gentle slope as seen from the city.

Contractors were hired by November and on December 21, 1859, the first sod was broken amidst great celebration, a fireworks display, and torchlight processions through town, as every property owner envisioned golden opportunities in the new, burgeoning capital. The cold and stormy weather, although not deterring the celebrants, was perhaps an omen of things to come.

As soon as winter released its icy grip, construction began in earnest. The intent was to have all three blocks completed by July 1862, a span of only two years, all for the paltry cost (even for those days) of $540,000.

The cornerstone of Centre Block was laid in September 1860, by the Prince of Wales, who later became King Edward VII. The inscribed cornerstone was suspended from a large semi-Gothic frame bedecked with garlands and topped by a crown and the Prince of Wales's feathers. Once the stone was lowered into position, the Prince made the requisite gestures with a silver trowel and tapped the stone three times with a mallet. Three cheers rang out for the Queen, then for the Prince, and then for the governor general. The architects, politicians, builders and other dignitaries were presented to the Prince amongst great pomp. There was an immense upwelling of optimism.

Problems

Almost before the celebrations died down, the grand plan began to unravel. When foundations were dug, it was discovered that the limestone bedrock of the Hill was full of fissures and cracks, so that considerable reinforcing was required. To confound matters, the Department of Public Works requested numerous changes to the original plans which, together with the foundation problems, drove the construction costs up dramatically. By some oversight the original plans did not include heat and ventilation, which had to be added. By September 1861, the entire budget was expended. The buildings were barely above their foundations.

As one witness wrote, "Of all the public buildings in Canada it can perhaps be concluded that the most hastily and badly planned were the first and most important of all: The Parliament Buildings of Canada."

Stone Work

Much of the work in constructing the Parliament Buildings involved stone cutting and stone masonry, which was done by hundreds of stone cutters and labourers working for about a dollar a day. The stones were cut with steam-powered machines at a separate site to the east of the Hill, with the finished stones hauled by horse cart to the site and then lifted into place using pulleys. Such physical labour without the aid of modern hydraulic equipment was both backbreaking and dangerous; a small infirmary near the Centre Block was constantly busy.

The mounting costs and delays caused an uproar amongst the frugal politicians who demanded explanations before releasing more funds. The government blamed the contractors for the wildly escalating costs; the contractors felt that the civil servants were making unreasonable demands. A major suspension of work ensued while, in typical Canadian fashion, a royal commission was appointed to find the causes. Although many problems were revealed, too much effort had already been invested. Construction of the three blocks was re-ordered but did not recommence until 1862 after a delay of nearly one year; the construction of the library restarted in 1870.

Completion

The East and West Blocks were completed and staff moved in during the fall of 1865. When the Centre Block was finished in 1866, Ottawa was still a rather small and rough-and-tumble lumber town, especially when compared to the more diverse centres of Toronto and Montreal. One contemporary neatly summed up the situation: "Ottawa is a small town with incongruously beautiful buildings crowning its insignificance."

The first parliament of the colony of Canada (Upper and Lower Canada combined) met on June 6, 1866, not realizing that this was to be their first and last meeting. When Confederation was realized a year later, in 1867, these buildings were selected for the new nation's parliament. This was a fine choice except that the original Centre Block had been planned for 130 MPs (65 from each of Upper and Lower Canada). With Confederation, 64 new seats were added, bringing the total to 194. Thus, the new Centre Block provided cramped quarters almost from the outset. The building became even more crowded when Manitoba, British Columbia, and Prince Edward Island entered Confederation the next decade.

The Library was not completed until 1876, so in the interim, books, records and other files had to be stored in attic rooms of the Centre Block. When finished the total cost of all the buildings was approximately $3,024,000 — almost six times the original budget.

The three original buildings were similar in style with their outer walls consisting of rough-hewn yellow sandstone taken from a quarry in Nepean Township, about 20 kilometres west of Ottawa. Each stone block has a different tint or tone so the affect is excellent; even today, the added grime and soot only serve to add an extra dimension to the texture. Red sandstone from Potsdam, New York, trims the doors and windows. The original grey slate roofs have been replaced with copper that has oxidized to a green. Wood trim was painted blue. The East and West Blocks, in particular, have a wonderful asymmetry, almost a mad

The East Block in winter — NATIONAL ARCHIVES OF CANADA PA43776

eccentricity; no two towers, nor two doorways and their broad elegant arches, are the same. Wings protrude here and there in an apparently random manner, yet it all comes together in a delightfully sensitive and inspiring manner. It must have been fun to design — you can almost see the architects and artisans chuckling as they worked. The interiors are also adorable, featuring exquisite carvings, paintings, murals, and stained glass.

The Original Centre Block

The original Centre Block, which was soon to be devoured by flames, was similar in design to the present one, with a few exceptions. The building had five storeys (versus six in the new Centre Block) and the House of Commons was in the middle (not in the western half as now). The most prominent difference is the tower in front was much shorter than the present Peace Tower and was, in fact, slightly shorter than Mackenzie Tower of West Block.

The East Block

The East Block was completed in 1865 and consists of three storeys and a basement. A wing was added on the northeast side in 1911 to create an enclosed courtyard. East Block, distinguished by the southwest tower with its caricature face watching over the Hill, is a beautiful building that captures the spirit of the Gothic style. The stonework has more colour than in Centre Block and the roof is adorned with fancy wrought-iron cresting.

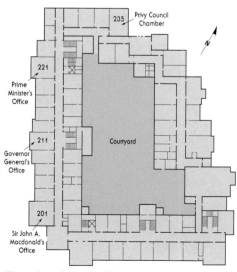

Floor plan of the East Block

The initial occupants were the departments of justice, finance, and agriculture. In addition, East Block housed the offices of the governor general, senior cabinet ministers, and the Privy Council (the cabinet). Canada's population was less than four million in 1865 and government was correspondingly much smaller than it is presently.

The building had central heat and running water. The original gas lighting was replaced by electricity in about 1900. Communication was by handwritten notes delivered by messengers who were summoned by bells. This method has been largely replaced by telephone and e-mail although some traditionalists still use the messenger service.

Major renovations have been made over time. Two main changes include the addition of a northeast wing in 1911, and a major renovation from 1976 to 1982 to modernize, remove asbestos, and to repair some of the historical damage done in earlier years. Queen Elizabeth officially reopened East Block in 1982. Special attention has been paid to preserving the historic atmosphere of the interior and for this reason, East Block is, in many ways, the most delightful of the three blocks. The interior features include arched windows, stained glass, and wood and wrought-iron balustrades.

Four of the rooms have been restored to their full Victorian splendour: the prime minister's office, the cabinet room, the governor general's room, and Sir John A. Macdonald's office. These can be visited during the summer months (see Chapter 11). The rest of the building is not open to the public.

The former prime minister's office is located in room 221 on the second floor. At first it was occupied by cabinet ministers, but every prime minister from Sir Wilfrid Laurier to Pierre Trudeau used this office. The room features a large wooden desk, a fireplace, a messenger-calling bell, wash basin, a chesterfield, and bookcases — all from the late 1800s. In 1976 the room was transformed into a museum and the prime min-

The Privy Council Chamber in the East Block   – HANS TAMMEMAGI

ister's office was moved into much more spacious quarters in the Langevin Block. The prime minister also has an office in Centre Block.

The former Privy Council Chamber, located in Room 235 in the northeast corner of the building, is a place of power — and of powerful history. Every cabinet from Confederation until 1976 sat around the large table in this room moulding Canada's destiny. Here the pros and cons of Confederation were debated; the decision to build a railway from sea to sea was made; measures to deal with Louis Riel's Red River Rebellion were formulated; the enfranchisement of Canadian women was hotly debated; heart-rending debates concerning conscription during the Great Wars ensued; the decision to replace the Union Jack with the distinctive Canadian maple leaf was reached; and methods of dealing with the FLQ crisis, including whether the War Measures Act should be invoked, were battled over. Meetings were held in secret, so it was truly a Privy (private) Council. It was not until the 1940s that secretaries were allowed to attend and keep minutes. The Chamber's anteroom served to store the oft-used statute books, and also as a banishment area for the nicotine-addicted when, on occasion, a particular prime minister chose to invoke a no-smoking rule. Since 1976, the Privy Council offices have been in the Langevin Block.

The former governor general's office is in Room 211 directly above the west portico, also known as the governor general's entrance. Here carriages of dignitaries arrived to meet the Queen's representative. Lord Dufferin was the first to occupy this room, which has been painstakingly restored to his era. All the government's codes and ciphers were kept here until 1928, and the Queen used the room for her office when she visited. The Governor General's New Year's Levee — when every "commoner" who comes to call is able to shake the hand of the governor general — was held here until 1928. The governor general's office moved to Rideau Hall in 1942.

The southwest corner office (Room 201) has been restored to the early Confederation era when it was occupied by Sir John A. Macdonald and subsequent cabinet ministers. Macdonald resided here as attorney general of Upper Canada from 1865 to 1867 and after Confederation as

Sir John A. Macdonald's office, East Block

– JANET BROOKS

prime minister, minister of justice and attorney general. The room has been beautifully preserved and includes its original furniture. Here, on May 6, 1870, Macdonald collapsed from gallstone complications and was too sick to be removed until almost a month later, when he was taken to the Speaker's chamber in Centre Block. On being told that his excruciating pain was caused by "a small gritty material," the fiery Scot quickly retorted, "Confound those Grits, I knew they would be the death of me yet."

Another important East Block tenant at the turn of the century was the Department of Finance. When the new wing was added, enormous vaults were included that housed prodigious amounts of gold and currency. The East Block was also equipped with an incinerator to burn old paper money. During the First World War, Britain paid for its war supplies from the United States in pure gold bullion. For security reasons, Canada was the intermediary and all Britain's gold passed through the East Block, where it was weighed, tabulated, and stored before being transferred to the United States. During the war, approximately 40 million ounces of gold passed through the basement vaults. Although the valuts were removed in the renovations of 1976, the massive doors remain.

Today, the East Block is occupied by cabinet ministers, senators and their staffs.

The Sean O'Sullivan Chapel in the southwest corner of the ground floor was dedicated in 1991 as a place for contemplation, prayer, and meditation. The chapel honours the memory of a young Conservative MP who left politics for the priesthood only

Massive doors to former vaults, East Block
– Hans Tammemagi

View of the East Block roof
– Hans Tammemagi

Inside the tower of the East Block. – HANS TAMMEMAGI

Stone walls in East Block tower – HANS TAMMEMAGI

Spiral staircase inside the southwest tower, East Block
– HANS TAMMEMAGI

A Geological Peek at the Parliament Buildings

The entranceway on the south side of the East Block at the west end offers an excellent overview of the different rock types used as construction material. The curb stones are grey granite while the steps are rough-dressed limestone. Most of the exterior walls are made of a yellowish Nepean sandstone with different weathering colourations which give them an attractive rugged, appearance. A very fine-grained, khaki-coloured sandstone from Wallace, Nova Scotia, surrounds the door and is also the medium for several nearby carvings. A red sandstone is used for the top of the Gothic arch and the circles above the door.

to die of cancer shortly thereafter. The room contains a carved wood altar and is used for weddings and memorial services, as well as for meditation.

The dominating southwest tower rises 45 metres and is capped by a wrought-iron terminal that rises another 15 metres on the top of this. Its windows form a caricature of a face whose down-turned, sad mouth provides a certain levity that may have been intentional — or perhaps not. The inside of the tower has never been heated or used and the walls are unfinished with supporting timbers exposed and chisel marks still preserved on the rough-hewn sandstone. A rickety, spiral steel staircase that seems to wind endlessly upward provides access to the top of the tower.

The West Block

The West Block comprises four storeys and was completed in 1865. A west wing and the Mackenzie Tower were added in 1874. The tower fell down shortly after it was constructed and had to be rebuilt, raising suspicion that some contractors were cheating on their work. A wing was added on the north side in 1905 to create an enclosed courtyard.

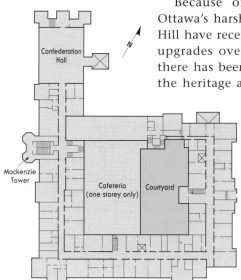

Floor plan of the West Block

Because of their age, heavy use, and Ottawa's harsh weather, the buildings on the Hill have received numerous renovations and upgrades over the years. In recent decades there has been a conscious effort to preserve the heritage and character of these magnificent buildings but, sadly, such efforts have not always been realized. By far the worst offence took place in 1960, when almost the entire interior of the West Block was gutted to make modern office space for parliamentarians. Unthinkably, most of the Victorian furnishings were destroyed in the process. Also, a vast area of the second floor was ripped out to create the huge Confederation Hall (Room 200) in the northwest corner where receptions are now held. For this reason, the interior of the West Block is the least interesting of those on the Hill.

Room 310, West Block   – Hans Tammemagi

Nor does the West Block have so rich a history as the other two blocks. Only one prime minister, Alexander Mackenzie (1873–1878), made his office in this block. The Mackenzie Tower was named in his honour and was the highest point on the Hill until the new Peace Tower was built. Mackenzie's office on the third floor is the only room in the entire building to have escaped the renovations of the past century

Spiral staircase in Mackenzie Tower, West Block
– Hans Tammemagi

relatively unscathed. The office, room 310, features carved pine panelling, a cathedral ceiling, large bow windows, a private washroom in its own little turret, and a secret passageway that permitted the prime minister to come and go with some degree of privacy.

On April 23, 1968, Pierre Trudeau, having just taken over the prime ministerial reins from Lester Pearson, dissolved parliament — and he did so in his own inimitable style. Following a caucus meeting in the West Block, he went to a meeting in what used to be Mackenzie's office on the third floor. He slipped out using the secret staircase built almost a century earlier and raced to Rideau Hall where he climbed over the back fence to avoid reporters. Meanwhile, his colleagues kept up the act by emerging at regular intervals from the office as though the meeting was still in progress. A few hours later, when the media finally caught up with Trudeau in the Centre Block, he evasively stated that he had been out to lunch. At 2:30 p.m., the new prime minister rose in the Commons and announced much to the surprise of all present, that he had met with the governor general and had requested him to dissolve Parliament and to have writs issued for an election.

The Library

The Library, directly behind the Centre Block and accessible via the Hall of Fame, is considered the most graceful building of its period and is thought by many to be the architectural gem of Canada. It was designed by Thomas Fuller and Chilion Jones, the architects of the original Centre Block. They attached the Library to the Centre Block in the same way that chapter houses are attached to many great English cathedrals. The distinctive round shape was undoubtedly inspired by the Round Reading Room of the British Museum in London, which influenced library design throughout the late nineteenth century. The Library was completed in 1876, nine years after Confederation. The opening was

A Dissenting Voice

Although there has been virtually unanimous praise for the Library, occasional dissenting voices have been heard. Probably the most prominent of these belonged to Sir John A. Macdonald, who confided to a visitor that the building might be best described as belonging to "the Cowbell style of architecture."

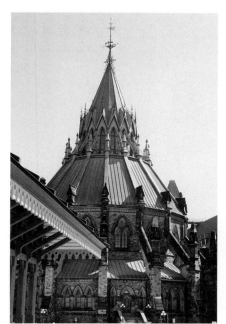

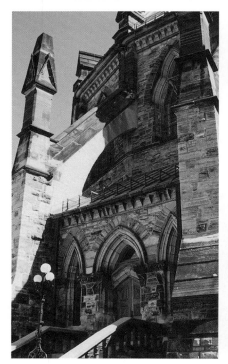

Views of the Library

– Hans Tammemagi

41

Interior of Library

– JANET BROOKS

The Library dome

marked by a gala ball hosted by the Earl and Countess of Dufferin, with 1,500 people crammed into every nook in the building.

Although it appears circular in shape, the Library is actually polygonal, consisting of sixteen massive stone walls of the familiar Nepean sandstone, each supported by a flying buttress. The building is 40 metres high and 27 metres in diameter. The roof was originally planned to be made of stone but, instead, was made of iron and later replaced with copper. The interior is dominated by a soaring cupola with windows at its base that permit natural light to diffuse through the beautiful interior. A white marble statue of Queen Victoria by Marshal Wood, an English sculptor, towers over the research tables. Three tiers of bookcases that rise three storeys in height line the walls. There are eight alcoves all exquisitely carved from Canadian white pine, and four stairways leading to the upper levels. The floors are inlaid with a variety of Canadian wood including ash, oak, cherry, and walnut. Although the Library escaped the fire of 1916, it suffered extensive water damage from a fire in its roof in 1952.

Although the exterior of the Library is Gothic, the interior is a Victorian

Interior of Library, 1898 — NATIONAL ARCHIVES OF CANADA PA8375

fantasy. Much of the warmth and beauty stems from the inspiring wood-carvings that adorn every corner. The entrance door from the Centre Block displays deeply cut figures of native animals including mink, fox, beaver, raccoon, heron, and eagle. Shelves and desks are made of Ontario white pine, hand carved with hundreds of Gothic patterns, much like the gargoyles and friezes done in stone throughout the Centre Block. Israel Page of Montreal was responsible for much of the woodcarving.

The Library's collection dates back to 1791 when Col. John Graves Simcoe brought with him from Britain the basic books for a legislative library for Upper Canada. In the following year, a legislative library was also established for Lower Canada. In 1841, when Upper and Lower Canada merged, so did their libraries. The Library now contains numerous literary treasures including an original edition of Champlain's voyages published in 1613, a near-complete set of the 1858 edition of *Jesuit Relations*, a set of *Birds of America* complete with notations by Audubon himself, and *Emily Montague*, the first novel published in Canada. Research in the library is supported by more than 600,000 books and a staff of over 250. The library has long outgrown this beautiful building and now has supporting branches in several other buildings in the Parliamentary Precinct.

All our great statesmen were at home in the Library at one time or another, and spent hours and hours conducting research in the beautiful wooden alcoves. When Sir Arthur Meighen, prime minister from 1920 to 1921 and also in 1926, was asked the secret of his quick rise to power, he answered quite simply, "The Library of Parliament." Senator Grattan O'Leary gave the following advice to young MPs, "Study and listen and wear a path to the Parliamentary Library."

Although the cost of the parliament buildings was high, the final result was worth it. With their flowing lines soaring heavenward, the buildings are the best example of Gothic architecture in North America.

Tunnels and Other Mysteries

Today, two tunnels join Centre Block to both the East and West Blocks, but in the past there were many more. The tunnel joining the West and Centre Blocks is relatively austere, but the link between East and Centre Blocks was refurbished in 1999 to luxurious standards, raising a brief furor in the press and in the House of Commons. Critics blasted the $3.6 million price tag that included the costs of a brass elevator, marble floors, and oak trim and handrails.

In the early days, waste water and sewage were drained from the East Block by a brick-lined tunnel which dumped into the Ottawa River. The practice lasted until 1876. There were undoubtedly numerous tunnels to service the other blocks, and to provide ventilation, most of which are uncharted on any of today's engineering plans. When the fire of 1916 raised fears about German sabotage, many of the tunnels were closed.

In 1950, excavation for an elevator in the East Block revealed a tunnel that was

Where does this sealed doorway lead?
– HANS TAMMEMAGI

not on the plans. For whatever reason, access to the tunnel was sealed without exploring and resolving the intriguing enigma of where it led. Perhaps it once joined the East Block and the Langevin Building. Or perhaps it was much older and was used by Colonel By's Royal Miners and Sappers as a secret route to a powder magazine. The Hill, to be sure, has its mysterious side.

Fire rages in the Centre Block, February 3, 1916   – NATIONAL ARCHIVES OF CANADA C-010079

Fire Rages!

ON the night of February 3, 1916, the temperature stood at –24° C and the snow crackled underfoot. It was a cold and bitter winter night as only Ottawa can suffer.

In the warmth of the Centre Block, the House of Commons was in session, debating a fisheries bill with the newly-appointed Deputy Speaker Edgar Rhodes presiding in the Speaker's chair. At approximately 8:50 p.m. Member of Parliament Francis Glass, who was browsing through some newspapers in the Reading Room, noticed smoke and quickly rushed out to sound the alarm. But it was too late. Fuelled by thousands of newspapers, flames soon engulfed the Reading Room and quickly spread into the corridors and the House of Commons chamber.

An alarm was called into a nearby fire station at 8:57 p.m. A scant three minutes later, fire fighters arrived at the scene. They must have been appalled at what they saw, for the original Centre Block, with its small rooms, wooden walls, heavy varnish, and oiled woodwork, had been transformed into a fire trap. It was already beyond saving.

In the House of Commons chamber next to the Reading Room, the debate had just finished. Members were privately chatting and tidying their desks when flames suddenly burst through the wall. Any effort to save papers or other relics, such as the mace, was abandoned as the members, pages, press, and visitors rushed for the exit. All were fortunate to escape the House without injury because only moments after their departure, flames raged through the chamber.

Prime Minister Borden had attended the debate earlier, but returned to his office to complete some work. A messenger rushed to warn him of the fire, and together the prime minister and messenger, crawling on

47

their hands and knees to keep below the smoke, found their way to a stairway and safety. Prime Minister Borden emerged into the freezing night without a coat or hat, as did all the other MPs, visitors, and staff. The prime minister then turned and went to his East Block office where he watched the blaze from a window.

Many MPs were working in their offices on higher floors and struggled to escape the flaming building. Two MPs quick-wittedly tied towels together to form a rope and climbed out a window and down the side of the building.

Fire fighters were called in from all over Ottawa, as well as from nearby towns. They were assisted by soldiers, for there was a fear of also losing the Library and the East Block. Search lights probed the dense smoke, refracting and reflecting from the bizarre and massive ice sculptures that formed by the water that poured from their hoses.

All through the night the big bell in the tower tolled on the hour, unaware of the inferno that surrounded it. Just after it struck the ten, long deep notes to indicate 10:00 p.m., a series of explosions rocked the night. The roof blew off and flames shot 30 metres into the sky. At 11:00 p.m., with the Centre Block in ruins, the bell announced the hour yet again. At midnight the tower clock struck eleven times, but before it could issue the 12th and final peal, it crashed to the ground.

A tattered picture of the Centre Block in flames, February 3, 1916
– City of Ottawa Archives CA7639

Saved by grace or good fortune, the solitary Library forms the backdrop for workers rebuilding the Centre Block.
– NATIONAL ARCHIVES OF CANADA PA130624

By a small miracle, the adjoining Library was saved through the quick-witted action of a guard who rushed to close the fire-proof iron doors connecting it to the Centre Block.

Due to the speed of the conflagration, virtually nothing was saved from the House of Commons. Along with the mace, all the chambers' furnishings, many paintings, thousands of records and files, and all the office furniture were destroyed. The fire took longer to reach the Senate, allowing time to save some paintings, furniture, and relics. These precious items sat forlornly outside in the freezing night, guarded by a lonely constable.

The painting of Queen Victoria by John Partridge was hurriedly cut from the frame and carried out by a police constable and A. H. Todd, a member of the senate staff. By coincidence, Todd's uncle, Alpheus Todd, rescued the same portrait when the Montreal parliament was burned down by a mob in 1849. Today you can admire this fine painting, in its new frame, in the Senate foyer on the west side of the entrance to the building.

In the end, it was a disastrous night. Not only did Canada lose its centre of government and one of the most beautiful buildings in the country, seven people perished. Mme. H. A. Bray and Mme. Louise Morin,

The new Centre Block is raised in front of the Library.   – National Archives of Canada C-38754

guests of the wife of the Speaker, were participating in a piano recital. In the midst of the performance, Speaker Albert Sévigny burst in and helped everyone in the Speaker's chambers get safely outside. Unfortunately, Mme. Bray and Mme. Morin went back inside to retrieve their coats and were trapped by the flames. Although rescue attempts were mounted, they were made in vain.

MP Bowman Law of Yarmouth, Nova Scotia, who had served in the House of Commons for more than 20 years, was trapped in his fifth-floor office and perished. Two security guards and two staff members also died. These seven unfortunate souls are now commemorated in the Hall of Honour.

However tragic, parliament had to continue; the country still needed to be governed. An emergency cabinet meeting was held at midnight in the Chateau Laurier. At 3:00 p.m. the next day, with embers on the Hill still warm,

Dinosaurs

Perhaps without the symbolism intended, the Senate chamber was placed in a hall previously used to display "fossils and leviathans."

a temporary parliament was established in the Victoria Museum (now the Canadian Museum of Nature). Within only three days, completely outfitted offices for the members were made ready in the museum galleries. Parliament was to operate here for the next three years.

As the First World War raged, many suspicious minds felt the fire was an act of German sabotage. Newspapers across the country were quick to sensationalize and raise tempers to a fevered pitch. *"Did Hun conspirators Start the Fire?,"* blared the February 4 headline in the *Ottawa Journal*. The Fire Chief did little to quell fears; and reported that in his opinion, "The fire was set and well set. I distinctly heard five explosions.... I am sure they were shells."

The results of an ensuing investigation were inconclusive, although it was (and still is) commonly understood that a careless smoker in the reading room was the real culprit.

Meanwhile, Canada, already suffering from the loss of many of its bravest sons and daughters overseas, began the painful task of reconstructing the majestic Parliament Building.

Construction of the new Centre Block

A New Centre Block Rises

A grieving and torn nation set to work to replace its most cherished building. From the ashes rose a mighty new edifice that was to become the home of Canada's parliament and a symbol of a growing, democratic nation. Reconstruction took place from 1916 to 1920, during and immediately following the Great War — a time when the country was struggling and resources were scarce.

At first it had been thought to use the walls and foundation of the gutted Centre Block, but closer examination revealed that they were not structurally sound. The entire building had to be razed, leaving the lonely Library in full view.

Work progressed well and the cornerstone of the new Centre Block was laid by Edward, Prince of Wales, on September 1, 1919. Putting many gloomy years behind them, more than 35,000 people came out to celebrate. After the ceremony, the Prince mingled with the veterans who had come back from "The War to End All Wars." In memory of the original Centre Block, its cornerstone was preserved and placed into the new building. It can be seen on the east side near the LaFontaine-Baldwin statue. The new building was formally opened in 1920.

Due to war-time shortages, the new Centre Block is more austere than the original. It is, however, bigger and more functional. Consisting of six storeys with a floor space of 30,500 square metres, it is one storey higher and about 50% larger in floor area than the original. The building has a stone structure with steel frame. Like its predecessor, the primary stone is Nepean sandstone with Ohio sandstone used for trim and decoration. The courts, chimneys, and penthouses utilize Wallace sandstone, a material not used in the earlier building. And the red Potsdam stone

53

Chapter **6**

Workers high above Centre Block
– NATIONAL ARCHIVES OF CANADA C38750

that framed the doors and windows of the first Centre Block was not used again as the architects felt it gave an uneven tone. Both the Centre Block, and the Peace Tower, completed seven years later in 1927, were designed by John A. Pearson of Toronto and J. O. Marchand of Montreal.

Although the Centre Block is best known as home to the House of Commons and Senate, there is much more. It contains reading and committee rooms, offices, a dining room, and is a living, evolving art gallery with an outstanding collection of paintings, stone and wood carvings, and stained-glass windows. In fact, the Centre Block is unique as it is the only government building in North America that has had such an extensive program of stone carving carried out over such a long period.

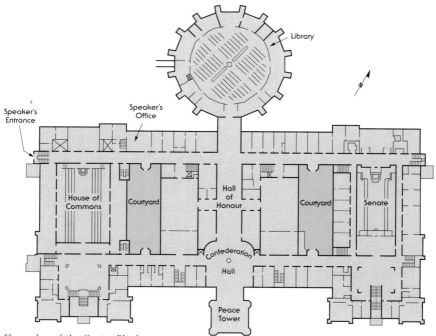

Floor plan of the Centre Block

House of Commons

The House of Commons is the focal point of Canadian government. With seating for 301 members of parliament, it is the largest chamber in the Centre Block and is elegantly furnished and decorated. The doors are

The House of Commons chamber   – ANDY SHOTT

The Speaker's chair in the House of Commons
– ANDY SHOTT

made of Canadian white oak. The ceiling towers 15 metres above the floor and is made of Irish linen decorated with floral emblems of the provinces that were hand painted after the linen was put in place. The cornice is gold leaf. Twelve stained glass windows illuminate the official flower of each province and territory. Designed by Dominion Sculptor Eleanor Milne and crafted by Toronto artist Russell Goodman, the windows were completed in 1973 and are considered to be the most beautiful stained glass anywhere in Canada.

The Speaker's chair at the north end of the chamber is an exact replica of the one in the House of

Commons in Westminster, England. Above the chair is the royal coat of arms. It was carved from an oak roof beam erected in 1397 in Westminster during the reign of Richard II. The chamber is furnished in moss green and the desks and panelling are of carved oak. Desks for each member of parliament are in neat rows along each wall with the government and opposition benches to the right and left of the Speaker, respectively, and separated by a length of two swords, as determined by British tradition.

The chamber is surrounded on all four sides by elevated galleries offering the public excellent views of honourable members and their activities. The two galleries along the sides are reserved for the guests of MPs, the prime minister, the Speaker, and the diplomatic corps. The press sit directly above the Speaker's chair. Public galleries, available on a first-come basis, are at each end of the chamber.

The mace on the Table of the House
– ANDY SHOTT

The large gold mace on the Table of the House in front of the Speaker's chair is a gift from the silversmiths of London. This symbolic piece was presented to Canada by the Lord Mayor of London in 1916 to replace the original that was destroyed in the fire. It contains the melted remains of the original.

The House of Commons foyer, located to the south of the chamber, is a popular place for media scrums. The walls of the foyer are lined with portraits of early prime ministers as well as a beautiful stone frieze carved by Eleanor Milne. The frieze depicts Canadian history from the Stone Age to the coming of the United Empire Loyalists. Portraits of more

Why a Mace?

In the Middle Ages, the sergeants-at-arms of the royal bodyguard wielded heavy round-headed clubs with protruding iron spikes. Capable of piercing armour, the mace was much feared and became a symbol of the king's power. Although far deadlier weapons are now available, the mace remains a symbol of the crown as vested in Parliament, as well as of the sergeant-at-arms' authority to maintain order and arrest miscreants. The mace is carried into the House chamber by the sergeant-at-arms who walks before the Speaker. When the House is in formal session, the mace rests on the Table of the House; when the House meets in committee (see Chapter 9), the mace rests beneath the Table.

recent prime ministers line the corridor from the foyer to the Hall of Confederation at the main entrance to Centre Block.

The mace cabinet   – ANDY SHOTT

Booze

MPs have been notorious for improving the eloquence of their speech by the application of alcoholic stimulants, sometimes to the point of rambling incoherence. The original Centre Block had a saloon located directly beneath the Speaker's chair and during session a steady procession of honourable members traipsed up and down the staircase. On occasion, members would become so inebriated and rowdy that the business of the House was brought to a standstill. The intake of alcohol is now taken more surreptitiously, with many MPs' offices equipped with well-stocked refrigerators.

Senate

The Senate, although smaller than the House of Commons, has its own special character and elegance. It contains 105 places for senators and is

Green Versus Red

Why is the House of Commons green and the Senate red? These traditional colours are rooted in the British parliamentary system and date back many centuries to the days when royalty and nobility were associated with red, and the common people, who sat on the grass, with green. Thus, the British House of Lords (our Senate) is known as "the red chamber," and the House of Commons as "the green chamber."

furnished in dark red with walnut desks and oak panelling. As befitting the upper class who traditionally sat in the British upper house, the Senate is more luxurious and ornate than the House of Commons. Ten large paintings display scenes from the First World War. The ceiling is composed of recessed glass panels adorned with emblems of Canada, France and Great Britain. Huge chandeliers, each weighing two tons, are suspended over the chamber. At the north end of the room a grand canopied chair, saved from the fire of 1916, sits regally on a raised dais and is used by the monarch or governor general at the opening of parliament. Many important ceremonies take place in the Senate, including the opening of parliament, the royal assent of bills, and the prorogation of parliament (these are described in Chapter 9).

Leading into the Senate is an elegant foyer that is lined with oil paintings of British kings and queens who have reigned over Canada, including George III and Queen Charlotte, a young Queen Victoria, King Edward VII, King George V, and Queen Mary. The last three are replicas of paintings that were destroyed in the fire of 1916. Above the oil works, and carved in the stonework, are the faces of some of the sculptors whose work adorns Parliament Hill.

The Senate in session, 1998

– MICHAEL BEDFORD

Confederation Hall

The main entrance to the Centre Block is located at the base of the Peace Tower. The doors lead into Confederation Hall (also known as the Rotunda), one of most beautiful places on the Hill. Circular in shape with a vaulted ceiling, it is a masterpiece of stone masonry consisting of a central column surrounded by eight outer columns, each intricately carved from Tyndall Stone, a beautiful mottled limestone from Manitoba that is rich with fossils. The top of each column fans out creating a dazzling array of stone arches that join with the central column to form the ceiling.

Confederation Hall — HANS TAMMEMAGI

The pillars are black marble, the floor both black and white marble. The central column is carved in an allegorical figure of Neptune and its base is set with a sixteen-point mariner's compass. The joining together of the arches from the different columns at the ceiling is architecturally symbolic of the provinces merging into a unified Canada.

The Hall of Honour

The Hall of Honour leads from Confederation Hall to the Library. The walls contain memorials to the seven men and women who died in the fire of 1916, and to the nurses who died in the First World War. Committee rooms lead off the Hall.

The Hall of Honour — NCC/CCN

A New Centre Block Rises

The Dining Room

The parliamentary dining room is situated in the northwest corner of the sixth floor. It is a graceful room with delightful views onto the Ottawa River, the Chaudière Falls, and Hull. Skylights add further natural lighting. Gourmet meals are prepared by a master chef. Although the room exudes friendly bonhomie, it is clearly divided into political territories. An alcove to the left of the entrance is reserved for the prime minister, an alcove to the right for senators. Each major party has an area where strategy and other confidential matters can be discussed in private. Mingling between parties and more public dining take place in the centre of the room. The restaurant is not open to the public. (More on the dining room in Chapter 11.)

Stone Carvings

The Centre Block is distinguished from other great Gothic buildings in the world by the stone carvings found in many nooks and crannies. The carvings, which draw unanimous praise, have been a labour of love for a series of sculptors over many decades. The variety of sculptures is breathtaking and almost bewildering in their range, including giant friezes,

Tyndall Stone

The primary decorative stone in Centre Block is a beautiful brownish-grey stone with a delicate mottling, "like frost ferns on a window pane," that adds to the dignity of Confederation Hall and the other grand hallways. Tyndall limestone, quarried at Garson, Manitoba, about 50 kilometres north-east of Winnipeg, is unique among building stones and is sometimes called the "tapestry stone." It was formed about 450 million years ago in the muddy bottom of Lake Agassiz, and is referred to, in geological terms, as the Upper Mottled Limestone of the Red River Formation of the Ordovician System.

Throughout Tyndall Stone are captured many representatives of ancient marine life. The most common fossils are corals, particularly the sunflower variety. Also found are brachiopods, gastropods, and cephalopods. Fossils of snails and nautiloids can sometimes reach giant proportions. The trilobite, the three-lobed crab-like creature that is the dominant form of the lower paleozoic, is only occasionally found.

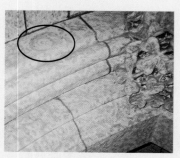

A cephalopod fossil in Memorial Chamber – HANS TAMMEMAGI

A good fossil cephalopod can be seen in the Memorial Chamber. Once you have entered turn around and look above the doorway arch and slightly to the left. Ask the tour guide or guards on duty for other good fossil locations.

Gargoyles and other stone carvings

Gargoyles were used in early Greece and Pompeii as water spouts to drain water from the parapet gutter of the roof. The term gargoyle later became restricted primarily to grotesque carved spouts of the Middle Ages. It is frequently — although incorrectly — applied to other grotesque beasts such as the chimeras of Notre Dame in Paris. The gargoyles of the Gothic period are usually grotesque birds or beasts sitting on their haunches near the edge of a roof and projected forward for several feet to throw rain-water away from the building. They were a characteristic of Gothic revival architecture and represent the imaginative and mythological spirit.

The best examples on the Hill are the four large gargoyles on the Peace Tower just below the clock face which snarl and sneer at walkers below; they were designed to be spouts for rain water. Other stone carvings include 12 musicians situated above the carillon on the Peace Tower. The carvings have been done with some conceit (or perhaps sense of humour) as the heads of the first official carvers themselves are found in the Senate foyer. The busts of Thomas Fuller and John A. Pearson, the architects of the first and second Centre Blocks, respectively, stare out from the main walls on either side of the Peace Tower (Fuller, with a grotesque body, is on the west side, and Pearson on the east).

Former Speaker, Gilbert Parent, inspects a grotesque
– Andy Shott

Stone carving outside main entrance to Centre Block
– Hans Tammemagi

the unicorn and lion that guard the main entrance, grimacing frightening gargoyles, and caricatures of politicians and some, even of the sculptors themselves. No visit to the Hill is complete without a careful inspection of these treasures. A self-guided tour of stone carvings is described in Chapter 11.

The Centre Block also contains many examples of excellent wrought-iron artisanship. Paul Beau of Montreal hand crafted the wrought-iron handles on the door of the House of Commons and all the fireplace accessories.

A New Centre Block Rises

The Peace Tower

– Hans Tammemagi

Peace Tower:
Memories of a War

THE Peace Tower is the crowning glory of Parliament Hill and forms a magnificent memorial to Canada's role in the First World War, with its tall Gothic lines symbolizing both victory and peace. Construction of the Tower began in 1920 — just after the Centre Block was finished — and was completed in 1927. The flagpole on top of the Tower is the highest point in the National Capital Region. A light mounted on top of the pole is turned on whenever the House of Commons is sitting.

The main entrance to Centre Block passes through graceful arches at the base of the Tower which are guarded by a stone carved lion and a unicorn. Above the arches are inscriptions; the one above the main doorway reads, "The wholesome sea is at her gates, her gates both east and west."

The Tower is a free-standing structure (that is, it is separate from, although attached to, Centre Block). It is made of Nepean sandstone that rises to a height of 90 metres. The tower contains the Memorial Chamber, the carillon, a clock, and an observation deck open to the public.

Memorial Chamber

The Memorial Chamber, in particular, was designed to commemorate the years of agony, suffering, and sacrifice of the First World War. This beautiful small room has been called "the holiest spot on Canadian soil," and conveys the dignity and grace of a Gothic cathedral.

Great wrought-iron gates guard the entrance and over the doorway are carved the heads of animals that served the troops during the war. The stones in the Chamber came from Canada's World War I allies: the

63

Chapter 7

pale white walls are of Chateau Gaillard and stone from France, the altar is white limestone from England, and the altar steps are black marble from Belgium. The floor is made of stone from the battlefields where Canadians fought and is inlaid with shell casings and inscribed with the names of major battles including Ypres, Mont Sorel, Vimy Ridge, Amiens, and the Somme. Stained glass windows are on three walls.

The Altar of Remembrance forms the centrepiece of the Chamber; it is carved with the arms of Canada and bears a gold-framed glass casket. The names of the 114,710 Canadians who died in combat outside Canada since 1867 have been inscribed by hand and are arranged alphabetically in eight Books of Remembrance. World War I and II comprise two volumes each. One volume from each war is always on the Altar in the casket. The pages are turned every morning at 11:00 in such a way that every name is visible at least once every year. Placed on side-altars are four volumes dedicated to those who fell in 1884–1902, which includes the Nile Expedition and the Boer War; those who perished while serving in the Merchant Navy; those who died in the Korean War from 1950–53; and to Newfoundlanders who fought and died from 1867 to 1949, before the colony joined Canada. Many people time their visits to Parliament Hill and the Memorial Chamber so they can see the name of someone special, perhaps a husband, wife, friend or relative, in the Book of Remembrance.

The poem "In Flanders Fields," by John McCrae, is carved into the east wall; a shiver will run down your spine as you read the lines in this peaceful spot and imagine the horror that he and his colleagues must have experienced when these ageless lines were written.

Carillon

In 1919, Frederick C. Mayer, the greatest living authority on carillons, had just completed a survey of the world's great carillons. He was therefore the perfect man to advise on the Canadian Carillon project. On seeing the wonderful setting with its commanding position, he enthusiastically announced that Canada would prove to have the finest carillon in the world.

Inaugurated on July 1, 1927, on Canada's sixtieth birthday, the music of the bells was broadcast across the nation. The carillon consists of 53 bronze bells ranging from 4.5 kg and 20 cm in diameter to 10,160 kg and 250 cm in diameter. With a total weight of 60 tonnes, the bells span 4.5 octaves. The bells were cast in the foundry of Gillett and Johnston in Croydon, England, and were tuned by paring away metal from the inside surface until the component notes were all in harmonious relationship. The bells remain stationary and are struck by steel clappers that are oper-

The Memorial Chamber — NCC/CCN

Carillon bells being delivered to the Peace Tower — National Archives of Canada, PA143969

Carillon bells in the Peace Tower and the carillon keyboard — Hans Tammemagi

ated, with some difficulty, by cables and pulleys from a keyboard that resembles a piano. The carillon is situated below the clock high in the Peace Tower, with the bells occupying two belfries and the keyboard in a little room in a floor between them.

Playing the carillon is no easy task. Gordon Slater, the Dominion Carillonneur, removes his wedding ring and wrist watch and dons a pair of sturdy fingerless gloves prior to each performance. When pressing the foot pedals for the dramatic and deep notes of the largest bells, he rises right off his seat.

The melodious chimes of the carillon drift over the Hill every weekday for fifteen minutes starting at 12:00. On Sunday evenings and major holidays the carillonneur plays an hour-long concert. The carillon also proclaims each hour and quarter hour with the same four-note chimes as Big Ben in London. The voices of the bells are also heard at other special occasions when Canadians celebrate, or pay tribute, or receive guests of honour.

> ### Ghost Sounds Sour Note
>
> The largest carillon bell is also the most temperamental. When it sounds a sour note the blame is placed on the ghost of former Prime Minister William Lyon Mackenzie King, whose name is inscribed on the bell and who was present when it was cast.
>
> When the carillon was completed, by happy chance there was a Canadian carillonneur, Percival Price, ready to assume the honour. It was he who made the Peace Tower carillon familiar to Canadians through programs that were broadcast across the country. In 1939, Robert Dunnell assumed the role of second Dominion Carillonneur. The present carillonneur is Gordon Slater. Today, concerts are also given by visiting carillonneurs who come from around the world to study and play the Peace Tower carillon.

Observation Deck

The observation deck, located below the large clock face, is open to the public and offers unparalleled views of Parliament Hill, Ottawa, Hull, and the Gatineau hills. To reach it you must first ascend in a unique elevator. Installed in 1981, it is the world's first two-directional lift. That is, it first rises vertically but then changes directions partway up and travels the rest of the way at 8 degrees off a vertical line.

The Clock

Immediately above the observation deck is the Peace Tower clock with its four huge 5-metre-diameter dials that display the time to people far around. To ensure punctuality on the Hill, the clock mechanism is remotely-controlled by the Dominion Observatory, which is located only a few kilometres south. There are four large gargoyles just below the clock face that serve as spouts for rain water.

Spring crocuses and the East Block

The Grounds
of the Hill

THERE is no more enjoyable way to wile away a sunny afternoon than to amble about the grounds of the Hill, watching the light play on the buildings with their rough stone walls, multiple entranceways, asymmetric designs, and soaring towers and roof lines. And you will not walk alone, for every breeze carries gentle whispers from the many prominent Canadians who have walked here in the past. Turning a corner you will suddenly meet one of these many ghosts, looming larger than life, silhouetted against the sky in mute bronze. Over a dozen statues populate the Hill; be sure to visit them. Seated at their feet, leaning against the sun-warmed granite, you will gain insight into Canada's history as well as into the personalities of those who have crafted our past.

In the early days the grounds of the Hill were barely more than rough dirt fields that did little to enhance the majestic Parliament Buildings. In 1873, the Department of Public Works hired Calbert Vaux, an architect from New York, to rectify this situation, and over the subsequent two years, a lovely green landscape took form that has remained much the same to this day.

The Buildings

The three magnificent Gothic buildings with their adjoining Library are the highlight of the Hill and you should take time to slowly circle each one, savouring the splendid architecture. Dominating the whole scene is the slender Peace Tower that draws the eyes skyward. Take your time to locate and enjoy the many stone carvings that adorn Centre Block. Test

Chapter 8

Southwest entrance to the East Block; a bishop's hat tops the wooden doors.
– Hans Tammemagi

your knowledge of Roman numerals on the cornerstone from the original Centre Block.

The buildings have a lightness and whimsy about them that will put a spring in your step and a song in your heart. A good example of this light-hearted style is the entranceway located on the south side of the East Block at the west end, modestly tucked away and little seen by visitors. It appears as though the architect ran wild, adding arch after arch of multi-coloured stones above the sturdy doors, dwarfing them into insignificance. The outcome looks like an ornate bishop's hat placed precipitously atop the stately wooden, double doors.

The three parliamentary blocks and an attractive wrought-iron fence with sandstone pillars enclose a large grassed space that is empty but for the Centennial Flame and Fountain. For more than 130 years, this quadrangle has been a gathering spot, drawing Canadians like a magnet whenever there is something significant to commemorate. This quadrangle has hosted sombre funeral processions, regiments of colourful marching guards, happy crowds packed like sardines on Canada Day, large ice sculptures, protestors shouting and waving placards, and dramatic sound & light shows.

View of the Hill from behind the Supreme Court   – Hans Tammemagi

And don't forget to stroll behind the Parliament Buildings. It is more serene, and you can admire the graceful lines of the Library — probably the most beautiful building in Canada — in relative peace. Just past the Library, the land tumbles abruptly over a steep cliff down to the glistening Ottawa River far below. You can sit in the cool shade of the Summer Pavilion, listen to the purr of friendly felines in the Cat Sanctuary (discussed later in this chapter), or look down on tiny boats slowly being lifted up the locks of the Rideau Canal.

Statues

My favourite pastime is to visit the statues and sit quietly at their feet, daydreaming of yesteryear and imagining the stories they could tell.

Here, in the order in which you may wish to tour them, is some information about the prime ministers and other heroes who are honoured in bronze. The locations of the statues are shown in the figure to which the numbers in the text below are keyed.

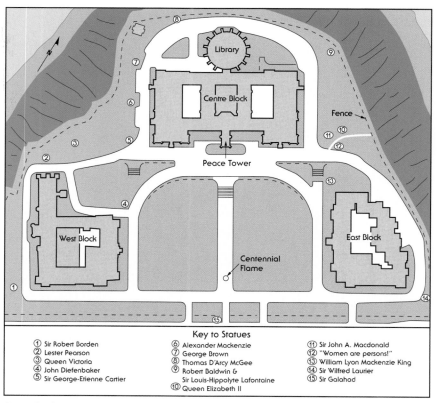

Key to Statues

① Sir Robert Borden	⑥ Alexander Mackenzie	⑪ Sir John A. Macdonald
② Lester Pearson	⑦ George Brown	⑫ "Women are persons!"
③ Queen Victoria	⑧ Thomas D'Arcy McGee	⑬ William Lyon Mackenzie King
④ John Diefenbaker	⑨ Robert Baldwin &	⑭ Sir Wilfred Laurier
⑤ Sir George-Etienne Cartier	Sir Louis-Hippolyte Lafontaine	⑮ Sir Galahad
	⑩ Queen Elizabeth II	

Grounds of the Hill showing statue locations

Statue of Sir Robert Borden   – HANS TAMMEMAGI

Sir Robert Borden (1) was the prime minister of Canada from 1911 to 1920. The sculpture shows Borden in casual repose. Born in Nova Scotia, he led the government through the difficult years of the First World War, bringing together a divided nation and effectively increasing industrial capacity to support the Allied effort. Much of this work was done in a temporary parliament due to the fire of 1916. Canada emerged from the war a more independent and respected country. In 1918, his government gave women the right to vote in federal elections.

Lester Pearson (2) was prime minister from 1963 to 1968. During his term of office he placed considerable emphasis on foreign affairs and did much to enhance Canada's reputation on the world stage. He served as president of the United Nations General Assembly and won the Nobel Peace Prize for his efforts in the Suez and as originator of the concept of UN Peacekeeping forces.

The Grounds of the Hill

The Queen Victoria statue   – HANS TAMMEMAGI

Queen Victoria (3) was the Sovereign of England and the British Empire from 1837 to 1901. In 1857, she chose Ottawa as the site for Canada's capital. A British lion, and a female figure representing Canada, adorn the base of this statue. After the statue was erected in 1901, it was noticed that certain parts of the lion were anatomically too correct. The scar from the incision to remove the lion's "cause of concern" can still be seen today. Ouch!

John Diefenbaker (4), prime minister from 1957 to 1963, was champion of the Prairie provinces. A skilled criminal lawyer, he spent his formative years in Saskatchewan. His term as prime minister was a stormy one as Canada struggled to define its role in the Cold War era. His government introduced the Canadian Bill of Rights.

Sir George-Etienne Cartier (5), one of the Fathers of Confederation, was Sir John A. Macdonald's Quebec counterpart. He was a leading proponent for a unified Canada and his statue, unveiled in 1885, was the first on the Hill. The statues of Macdonald and Cartier are placed symmetrically on each side of Centre Block.

Alexander Mackenzie (6) was Canada's second prime minister and served from 1873 to 1878. Mackenzie was a stonemason and bid on the construction of the Parliament Buildings. His government established the Supreme Court of Canada and introduced the first secret ballot elections in Canada.

George Brown (7) was one of the Fathers of Confederation. His government helped form the "Great Coalition" of the 1860s which led to Confederation. A scroll at the base reads, "Government by the people, free institutions, religious liberty and equality, unity in progress of confederation."

Statue of George Brown, a Father of Confederation — HANS TAMMEMAGI

The Statue of D'Arcy McGee — HANS TAMMEMAGI

Thomas D'Arcy McGee (8), also a Father of Confederation, was renowned for his eloquent and powerful oratory and his fervent support for a united Canada. An Irish patriot, he fled the Emerald Isle in 1848 disguised as a priest. He at first lived in the United States but then moved to Montreal where, in 1858, he was elected to represent the riding of Montreal West. He attended the Charlottetown and Quebec conferences that led to a confederated Canada. McGee is the only Canadian member of parliament to have been assassinated. A late night session at the House of Commons ended at 2:00 a.m. on April 7, 1868. McGee then descended to the House of Commons bar where he lit a cigar with his chief, Sir John A. Macdonald, chatted a while and then departed wearing an overcoat and a new white top hat. As he was inserting the key into the lock of Mrs. Trotter's boarding house on Sparks Street, he was shot through the head from behind. The country was outraged and rewards were posted for the assassin. Patrick Whelan, a member of the Fenians (a radical organization founded in New York in 1857 to seek independence for Ireland), was captured and hanged. Today, a small plaque at 142 Sparks Street marks the location where Mrs. Trotter's boarding house once stood.

Robert Baldwin and Sir Louis-Hippolyte Lafontaine (9) were pre-Confederation architects of responsible, democratic government. This is the only statue featuring two people.

Robert Baldwin and Sir Louis-Hippolyte Lafontaine   – HANS TAMMEMAGI

The Grounds of the Hill

Queen Elizabeth II astride "Centennial"   – Hans Tammemagi

Queen Elizabeth II (10) is shown astride her horse, "Centennial." Queen Elizabeth has reigned over Great Britain and the Commonwealth since 1952.

Sir John A. Macdonald (11) was one of the Fathers of Confederation and Canada's first prime minister. His vision of a nation united from sea to sea was the driving force behind the confederation of provinces. John A. was a lawyer and practiced in Kingston until elected to parliament at age 29. In Ottawa, he lived in Earnscliff on Sussex Drive, now the residence of the British High Commissioner. His statue was crafted by Leblanc-Barbedienne of Paris.

"Women are Persons!" (12), is the most recent — and the most entertaining — statue on the hill. On October 18, 2000, the larger than life statues of Emily Murphy, Henrietta Muir Edwards, Louise McKinney, Nellie McClung, and Irene Parlby were inaugurated on the anniversary of the landmark court ruling which allowed Canadian women into the Senate. The bronze monument recreates the scene of the five women celebrating their court victory after successfully fighting to have women legally recognized as "persons" under federal law. Even though women got the federal franchise in 1918, they did not win the right to sit in the Senate until 1929, after considerable legal wrangling that was finally decided in the British Privy Council.

"Women are Persons!"   – HANS TAMMEMAGI

William Lyon Mackenzie King (13) was prime minister from 1921 to 1930, and 1935 to 1948. Scowling and squinty-eyed, this statue captures the odd and sometimes suspicious personality of Canada's longest-serving prime minister (22 years). Generally considered the most fascinating and eccentric of our federal leaders, King was the grandson of William Lyon Mackenzie, leader of the 1837 Upper Canada Rebellion. He possessed a sharp intelligence and guided Canada through much of the Great Depression and the Second World War. King's government introduced the country's first social programs, including the Canada Pension Plan, unemployment insurance, and family allowance. When he died in 1950, he bequeathed his house in Ottawa and his estate at Kingsmere in the Gatineau hills to Canada. Both are now museums and the Kingsmere residence is home to the speaker.

Sir Wilfrid Laurier (14) was a Montreal lawyer who became the nation's first francophone prime minister. He served from 1896 to 1911. His home in Sandy Hill was subsequently used by his successor William Lyon Mackenzie King. It is now a museum.

Statue of Sir Galahad, dedicated to Henry Harper

– Hans Tammemagi

Sir Galahad (15). This statue commemorates Henry Harper, Assistant Deputy Minister of Labour, who lost his life in a vain attempt to save a fellow skater, Miss Bessie Blair. Miss Blair was the daughter of the Minister of Railways and Canals. She fell into the icy Ottawa River on December 6, 1901. William Lyon Mackenzie King, a close friend of Harper, headed up the drive to erect the statue and chose the inscription, from Tennyson's *Idylls of the King*, "Galahad ... cried 'If I lose myself, I save myself.'" A few years later, shortly after entering politics and just prior to his maiden address to the House, King placed ten white roses at the base of this statue.

Many other statues are found inside the parliamentary buildings as well as in other locations in the Parliamentary Precinct. Some statues are even harder to find as they are buried deep inside government warehouses, including the somewhat infamous statue of Arthur Meighen, described by John Diefenbaker as "the greatest monstrosity ever produced, a mixture of Ichabod Crane and Daddy Longlegs."

Centennial Flame

The Centennial Flame — JANET BROOKS

As the second hand ticked into January 1, 1967, Prime Minister Lester Pearson first lit the Centennial Flame which now burns endlessly in a fountain directly in front of Centre Block near Wellington Street. Fuelled by natural gas from Alberta, it is a symbolic light that leads the way into Canada's second full century of Confederation. Just as Canada rises above the waters of three oceans, so too does the flame which burns above the water of the fountain. The shields of all the provinces and territories line the perimeter along with the years they joined Confederation.

The West Block as seen from the Summer Pavilion in 1936
– National Archives of Canada, PA12636

Personalities and Protesters

A favourite pastime is to try and catch a glimpse of the prime minister or some of the well-known cabinet ministers and MPs. One good spot to wait is just outside the House of Commons entrance to the Centre Block, where a fleet of limousines hover, awaiting the arrival of their respective dignitaries.

The Hill attracts all kinds of protesters and activists trying to grab the attention of politicians — not to mention 15 minutes of media fame. The grounds in front of the Centre Block occasionally turn into a frenzy of waving placards, milling and pushing people, policemen with batons, and police horses towering over the throngs. The clamour of loud-speakers and voices reverberate off the sandstone walls. Increased security is a good clue that something interesting is about to happen.

Summer Pavilion

Built in 1877 and designed by Department of Public Works chief architect, Thomas Seaton Scott, this delightful wooden pavilion was once the

The Library as seen from the pavilion — JANET BROOKS

The Grounds of the Hill

scene of lavish parties thrown by the speaker, complete with rugs, tapestries, gourmet food and fine wine. Sadly, the pavilion was demolished in 1956. No record of its plans remain. However, it was rebuilt from collective memory in 1993 with funds from the Canadian Police Association and the Canadian Association of Chiefs of Police. In March 22, 1994, it was dedicated as a police memorial; services for slain police officers are held in this beautiful spot to the northwest of the Centre Block.

The Cat Sanctuary

By the edge of the cliff to the north of the West Block is an unusual place: a cat sanctuary. In the late 1970s, Irene Desormeaux started a home for Ottawa's stray cats. Dozens of them, as well as a few friendly squirrels, wander among the bushes and trees surrounding a row of brightly painted kitty kennels behind the wrought-iron fence. All the cats are neutered for health and stability and inoculated against rabies and feline distemper. They pose no hazard to the public, and many civil servants spend their lunch breaks on nearby benches with purring felines in their laps. In 1987, Desormeaux passed away and her duties were taken over by René Chartrand, who is known as the "Cat Man of the Hill." The annual cost of $6,000 to maintain the sanctuary is met with private contributions.

René Chartrand, the Cat Man of Parliament Hill with feline friend   – Hans Tammemagi

The cat sanctuary

Noon-Day Gun

Beside the cat sanctuary stands the now-silent noon-day gun, once part of one of Ottawa's most cherished traditions. The nine-pound muzzle-loader cannon was fired at exactly noon every day to establish the correct time. It was first discharged from Parliament Hill in 1869, but after the fire of 1916, was moved to Major's Hill park. The practice was discontinued in 1994, and the gun was returned to this spot.

Lovers' Walk

When the Hill was still a barrack ground for Colonel By's ditch-digging troops, water was hauled from the Ottawa River by wagon. The cart path through the trees became a popular walkway and benches were installed so strollers could enjoy the vistas of the river and the Gatineau hills. The dream-like glade in the heart of the city became immensely popular and served Ottawa much as Dufferin Terrace serves Quebec City.

With true bureaucratic resolve, Prime Minister R. B. Bennett closed the walk in the 1930s, fearing that it might become a magnet for vagrants and miscreants. Although Lovers' Walk is long gone, a promenade behind the Parliament Buildings along the cliff edge, particularly at sunset, still offers wonderful, peaceful panoramas.

The Grounds of the Hill

The House of Commons in session; 35th Parliament. Prime Minister Chrétien is standing
– THE LIBRARY OF PARLIAMENT

Parliament & Politics:
Steering The Ship of State

THERE has always been an inherent cynicism about political systems and about the politicians who stride the corridors of power. A few quotations on the topic should suffice:

> *Politics is not the art of the possible. It consists of choosing*
> *between the disastrous and the unpalatable.*
> — JOHN KENNETH GALBRAITH

> *Politicians are the same all over. They promise to build bridges,*
> *even where there are no rivers.*
> — NIKITA KRUSCHEV

> *All politics are based on the indifference of the majority.*
> — JAMES RESTON

> *He knows nothing and thinks he knows everything.*
> *That points clearly to a political career.*
> — GEORGE BERNARD SHAW

> *Politics is perhaps the only profession for which*
> *no preparation is thought necessary.*
> — ROBERT LOUIS STEVENSON

Cynicism aside, the political system is a vitally important part of society and democracy; it is something all citizens must understand. In this chapter we look at Canada's federal parliament and see how it works.

Chapter 9

Parliament Hill is the centrepiece of our democratic system, and here within the sandstone walls you can see it in action.

Anyone who has witnessed the heated and often acrimonious shouting matches of Question Period will understand why "parliament" is derived from the French word, *parler*, to talk. Indeed, one might wonder how anything but talking gets accomplished on the Hill.

But first impressions are deceiving for the House of Commons is the vehicle through which the will of democracy finds expression and is made effective. It is this institution, above all others, that represents, and speaks for, the people of Canada.

The most important feature of government is that it is a democracy, designed and established to serve the people of this country and to be responsive to their wishes — not an easy task considering the size and diversity of this nation. Nevertheless, the system has, to a large degree, protected the rights of individuals and minorities, avoided the abuse of power, and resulted in a good standard of living.

Fundamental Principles

Canadian democratic government is based on three basic principles: it is representative, responsible, and bound by law.

A representative government means that people are elected to speak and act on behalf of larger groups called constituencies. These representatives, called Members of Parliament (MPs), sit in the House of Commons. All parts of the country are represented; every Canadian has a representative speaking on his or her behalf in the House.

Second, the government is responsible to the electorate, that is, the Canadian people who elect it. The executive who initiate laws, namely the prime minister and cabinet ministers, must have seats in the House. If they cannot retain the support and confidence of the House (and therefore, the Canadian people), they must resign or dissolve parliament, letting voters resolve the issue at the ballot box.

The third principle is the government itself is bound by the rule of law and the Constitution. All acts of government must be based on law passed by parliament and not on the whim of whomever is in power. The prime minister and cabinet ministers are under the same legal restrictions as the constituents who elect them. The main way of ensuring this supremacy of law is by allowing all people the right to appeal to the courts for protection, and by ensuring that the courts are fair and independent of outside influence.

Before we look at the parliamentary system in more detail and see how laws are made and Canada is governed, we should note that everything on the Hill bears a British influence. The basic parliamentary system was designed after the British House of Commons and House of Lords, and many of the procedures, rituals, and traditions have their roots in Westminster. The rituals have, however, been reshaped and have evolved over many decades so they have taken on their own distinctive, Canadian character.

The figure below highlights the key components of Canadian government: the prime minister and cabinet (the executive), the House of Commons, the Senate, and the governor general. The remainder of this chapter looks at this system in more detail.

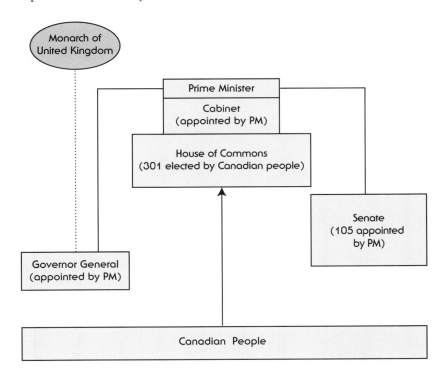

Prime Minister

The prime minister is the most powerful person in federal government and is the image or symbol of government. He or she chooses the cabinet and takes personal responsibility for government policy. The prime minister is the leader of the winning party and is elected by members of that party at a leadership convention. He or she has two offices: one in the Centre Block, the other in the Langevin Building where the prime ministerial staff is located. The prime minister has a luxurious residence at 24 Sussex Drive, a short distance to the east of the Hill.

Prime Ministers of Canada

Rt. Hon. Sir John Alexander Macdonald	1867–1873 & 1878–1891	Conservative
Rt. Hon. Alexander Mackenzie	1873–1878	Liberal
Rt. Hon. Sir John Joseph Caldwell Abbott	1891–1892	Conservative
Rt. Hon. Sir John Sparrow David Thompson	1892–1894	Conservative
Rt. Hon. Sir Mackenzie Bowell	1894–1896	Conservative
Rt. Hon. Sir Charles Tupper	1896–1896	Conservative
Rt. Hon. Sir Wilfrid Laurier	1896–1911	Liberal
Rt. Hon. Sir Robert Laird Borden	1911–1920	Conservative
Rt. Hon. Sir Arthur Meighen	1920–1921 & 1926	Conservative
Rt. Hon. William Lyon Mackenzie King	1921–1926 1926–1930 & 1935–1948	Liberal
Rt. Hon. Richard Bedford Bennett	1930–1935	Conservative
Rt. Hon. Louis Stephen St. Laurent	1948–1957	Liberal
Rt. Hon. John George Diefenbaker	1957–1963	Progressive Conservative
Rt. Hon. Lester Bowles Pearson	1963–1968	Liberal
Rt. Hon. Pierre Elliott Trudeau	1968–1979 & 1980–1984	Liberal
Rt. Hon. Charles Joseph Clark	1979–1980	Progressive Conservative
Rt. Hon. Martin Brian Mulroney	1984–1993	Progressive Conservative
Rt. Hon. Avril Phaedra (Kim) Campbell	1993–1993	Progressive Conservative
Rt. Hon. Joseph-Jacques Jean Chrétien	1993–	Liberal

Painting of Prime Minister
Wilfrid Laurier, 1897
– NAC, C123424

The prime minister of Canada, more so than the President of the United States, has considerable control over appointments and the bills that get enacted into law and thus can mould the government in his or her fashion. For example, the prime minister appoints the governor general, senators, the cabinet and many other government and patronage positions including deputy ministers and the heads of Crown Corporations such as the Canadian Broadcasting Corporation (CBC). Due to the enormous amount of power vested in this position, it might be said that Canada has a prime-ministerial system of government.

There have been 20 prime ministers from Confederation to 2002. Sir John A. Macdonald was the first; Kim Campbell has been the only woman to date. Two parties have shared power for the entire period of Confederation. By coincidence, they have held office almost exactly the same number of years.

The Prime Minister's Office (PMO) is the centre of power in the country and forms the hub around which government revolves. At the beginning of Confederation, the prime minister had one secretary and answered his own mail. What a difference a century makes. Now the prime minister's staff consists of more than 100 people. Their job is to write the prime minister's speeches, organize his schedule, "spin" his image, get him re-elected, and provide general support. The PMO staff are appointed by the prime minister and they resign when he or she is defeated. As might be expected, there is occasionally some friction and jealousy between the cabinet and the PMO.

The Cabinet and Privy Council Office

The cabinet, led by the prime minister, is known as the Executive and wields the most power and influence in Canadian government. The executive provides leadership for the country by initiating and creating policy and supervising its execution. All government bills are initiated and approved by cabinet before they are introduced to parliament.

The cabinet wields power not only by introducing bills, but also by issuing Orders in Council. Thousands of Orders are issued annually and although most deal with routine matters, such as appointments of deputy ministers and other civil service positions, contracts, and administration of departments, some also deal with matters of greater substance, such as the appointment of judges. Orders in Council are necessary to allow the smooth, day-to-day functioning of parliament, and the country.

The cabinet has approximately 30 ministers and most of them have "portfolios," that is, they are in charge of specific government departments such as finance, environment, foreign affairs, and agriculture. Sometimes there are Ministers Without Portfolio who are not in charge of any department, or Ministers of State, who are in charge of particular sections of departments. By custom, every province must be represented by at least one minister.

The Privy Council consists of all present and past cabinet ministers, although only the former ever meet formally. Thus, the cabinet is a subset of the much larger Privy Council. The Privy Council Office is the administrative arm of the cabinet. Its duties include organizing cabinet meetings, keeping minutes, and coordinating cabinet initiatives. In addition, it oversees and manages the federal civil service, including all federal departments such as justice, agriculture, and environment. The Privy Council Office has a staff of over 400, who are housed in the

Langevin Building. It is headed by the Clerk of the Privy Council, the most powerful civil servant in the federal bureaucracy.

Everything that occurs in the House and Senate is public information; all debates are reported in *Hansard* (the official "minutes" of parliament) and by reporters in the Press Gallery. But cabinet meetings are mostly confidential and are conducted in secret. Although cabinet meeting discussions may be sharp and acrimonious, once a decision is reached the differences are set aside and the cabinet presents a united party front to parliament and the country.

House of Commons

The official and symbolic centre of power in the country rests here. The main responsibility of the House is not as an initiating body — this is the role of the cabinet — instead its function is one of review, approval, and criticism. The House takes the proposals put forth by the cabinet and places them under its microscope, amending them if necessary, before giving its assent.

Both the House of Commons and the Senate can introduce legislation, and both bodies must pass the legislation before it becomes law. But the House of Commons holds the purse strings, and only the House may introduce financial legislation and set the federal budget.

There are 301 members of parliament who are elected to represent the people of their constituencies. The constituencies are divided among the provinces according to rules that are based on population but with some allowances for less populated provinces. The constituencies are adjusted by an independent commission every ten years after the national census has been taken.

The representatives the public vote for belong to political parties, which play important roles in ensuring the parliamentary system functions smoothly. Without parties, it would be difficult to form a cohesive cabinet, choose a prime minister, or ensure passage of important bills. The principal parties in today's parliament are Liberal, Progressive Conservative, New Democratic, Canadian Alliance, and the Bloc Quebecois. The party which wins the majority of seats in the House of Commons can control the voting and, hence, set the agenda for the country. The majority party is often referred to as the governing party, or the government. The leader of the majority party becomes the prime minister.

Elections must be held every five years or less. The majority party sits on the west side of the chamber on the Speaker's right. The opposition parties sit on the east side with the largest party in opposition closest to the Speaker.

The adversarial method is a fundamental part of the British parliamentary system; opposition parties can question, delay, amend, or possibly block bills which they oppose. The constant play of opposing forces on national issues is intended to expose the flaws in proposed legislation and the always ensuing debates help the public better understand issues of relevance. The opposition also provides some protection against the majority party monopolizing power.

Parliament is a "talking place," where freedom of speech is central. Parliamentarians can say anything they please within the two chambers or in committee rooms, but this privilege does not extend to the corridors or press conferences. Thus, the speeches and debate inside the House are often more stinging and insulting than statements to the press outside the protected walls, where libel suits can arise. Members can not be arrested for civil suits while parliament is sitting, or for forty days before or after a session.

The business of parliament is conducted according to complex rules that are based on traditions, many going back centuries. These rules are spelled out in 159 Standing Orders. A knowledge of points of order, how to make motions, introduce bills, and the mechanisms of standing orders is indispensable in the working day of members of parliament and senators. The clerk is the ultimate interpreter of these arcane rules. The Speaker, in particular, must know the rules so he or she can adjudicate debates fairly. The Speaker always relies heavily on the clerk.

As much of the work of government is done in committee, the attendance for debates in the House is sometimes quite small; only a quorum of 20 MPs is necessary to conduct debate.

The parliamentary year is divided into three regular sitting periods: the fall, winter, and spring semesters. The House hours vary during the week as follows:

The Good Ol' Days

Parliament initially sat for only four months each year. Departments were run by civil servants who worked from 9:30 a.m. to 4 p.m. They had two hours each day for lunch. Although the work week included Saturday mornings, on Thursday afternoons it was customary for wives to visit and stay for tea. Government was informal, as evidenced by the fact that cabinet did not keep an agenda or minutes until 1940. Today, members log long, gruelling hours trying to satisfy their constituents and fulfill their parliamentary obligations.

Mondays:	11 a.m. to 6 p.m.
Tuesdays:	10 a.m. to 6 p.m.
Wednesdays:	2 p.m. to 8 p.m.
Thursdays:	10 a.m. to 6 p.m.
Fridays:	10 a.m. to 4 p.m.

On Mondays, Tuesdays and Thursdays, from 5:30 to 6 p.m., five MPs can each make a four-minute speech to voice their opinions. The responsible minister has two minutes to respond, if he or she chooses to do so.

Question Period, a uniquely Canadian

tradition, is one of the most exciting events to witness when you visit the Hill. Forty-five minutes are set aside each day so opposition members can question the government. Questions usually revolve around the hot issues of the day and are invariably "loaded," as the opposition tries to embarrass a cabinet minister, who in turn tries to defend his or her actions and make the opposition member out to be the real fool. This give and take can range from witty and entertaining, to vicious and rude. Either way, it allows the government to be challenged, which is an important part of our democratic process. Question period is from 2:15 to 3:00 p.m. on Mondays to Thursdays and from 11:15 to 12:00 noon on Fridays.

A Boisterous Debate

In the early days of Confederation, the House was often quite unruly, no doubt assisted by the saloon below, to which the honourable members could make forays during prolonged debates. In the spring of 1878, the House of Commons was arguing over the dismissal of the government in Quebec by the lieutenant governor of the province. The situation soon got out of hand and led to scenes more suiting a lunatic asylum than a distinguished House of Commons.

Members hammered at desks, blew on tin trumpets, imitated the sounds of barn-yard animals, sent up balloons, threw firecrackers, and occasionally threw books at opposing colleagues. The babble of voices was so loud that neither the Speaker nor the member who had the floor could be heard. Every so often, some member would start up a song and then the whole House would join in. Despite the fact that the speaker had exhausted his subject, he kept the floor by quoting passages from law books, books of poetry, philosophy, and humour. Chaos punctuated the scene only to ebb slowly away as the members became tired, only to erupt again with renewed frenzy.

One speaker used up his time by reading the entire British North America Act in French, making humorous remarks on each clause. A party of members organized an impromptu band and began to play a species of music that was more discordant, if possible, than the voices and banging on desks that accompanied it. Any serious efforts to restore decorum to the proceedings were met with roaring, hooting, howling, whistling, singing, stamping, shouting, caterwauling, and desk thumping. In this merry vein, the House continued its debate non-stop for 27 hours.

Such a scene was not to be witnessed again on the Hill until 1990, when the Liberal members of Senate staged a raucous filibuster to delay the passage of the Goods and Services Tax bill.

A session of the House can end in three ways. It can be adjourned, that is, put on hold or recess anywhere from a few hours up to a few days. A session can also be prorogued, that is, formally closed, killing all proposed bills that are in progress. This is how the fall, spring, and winter sessions are ended when no election is to be held. A session can also be dissolved, and would only reconvene after an election.

Speaker

The Speaker, who represents all members of the House of Commons, is one of the most influential people in the federal parliament. The Speaker presides over the deliberations of the House, represents it in external matters, and most important, rules on questions of procedure. All speeches and questions must be directed to the Speaker and not to the person actually being addressed. As manager of the House of Commons with responsibility for an annual budget that exceeds $250 million, the Speaker can also be viewed as a chief executive officer. As the representative of the House, the Speaker attends international meetings of parliamentarians and welcomes dignitaries and celebrities ranging from royalty to Boy Scout delegations.

Originally, the Speaker was appointed by the prime minister, but since 1986 he or she has been elected from amongst the MPs in a free vote. The Speaker sits in a magnificent raised chair at the north end of the chamber, which is equipped with controls so that the microphones of any unruly MP can be turned off. Jeanne Sauvé, the first female Speaker, had a small elevator installed in the seat so she could raise herself to a more stately height. Four Latin mottos are inscribed on the left arm of the chair to inspire the Speaker: "Neither by entreaty nor gifts;" "Liberty lies in the laws;" "Envy is the enemy of honour;" and "Praise be to God."

The Speaker's office in 1931   – National Archives of Canada, C3353

Three more mottos are inscribed on the right side: "Mindful and faithful;" "The hand that deals justly is a sweet-smelling ointment;" and "A mind conscious of the right." Hidden at the foot of the chair is a small television screen by which the clerk sends messages and information. The Speaker does not vote except to break a tie. In keeping with British tradition, the Speaker wears a tricorn hat, black suit, white collar with tabs, a black silk robe, and white gloves.

Former Speaker Gilbert Parent leading the Speaker's parade.   – ANDY SHOTT

Each sitting of the House is preceded by the Speaker's procession, a charming ritual. Led by three constables and the sergeant of arms bearing the mace, the Speaker walks from the Speaker's office down the Hall of Honour to the Rotunda, and then to the House foyer and the chamber. The speaker is followed by a page, the clerk and assistant clerks.

In recognition of the importance of the position, the Speaker is provided with a residence at Kingsmere in the Gatineau hills; the Speaker also keeps a small apartment in the Centre Block. In 2001, Peter Milliken was elected the 34th Speaker.

House Leader

Each party in the House chooses a house leader (not to be confused with the party leader), who negotiates the Commons timetable with the other house leaders, determines which MPs will speak, supervises the whip, and is the tactician for the caucus. The government party's house leader is invariably a cabinet minister and is given the honorary title of President of the Privy Council.

Whips

Each party selects one MP to "whip" his colleagues into shape so they vote along party lines and are present for crucial votes. The whip plays an important role in ensuring the governing party remains in power. Responsibilities include knowing where members of the party are at all times and understanding their opinions on various bills. The whip must comprehend the grievances of party MPs, especially backbenchers, and must be able to smooth out any discontent in an effort to maintain party solidarity. To add muscle to this position, the whip allocates office space and decides who will sit on committees.

Caucus

Each party has a caucus consisting of all its elected members. Each caucus meets weekly to discuss policy issues, review their past week's perform-ances, and develop tactics to be employed in the House and Senate for the following weeks. Although most governing party policy is decided in the cabinet, the caucus provides a forum for backbenchers to voice their opinions. For the non-governing parties, the caucus provides an impor-tant arena for discussing strategy and policy. As caucus meetings are closed to the media and public, they are often lively, even rowdy.

Senate

In the days leading up to Confederation, the Senate was a critical topic in the negotiations that brought together the three disparate regions of Ontario, Quebec and the Maritimes. In particular, the less populated colonies of Nova Scotia and New Brunswick were adamant that they needed the protection of a Senate with its equal, rather than population-based, representation. Without the Senate there might not have been a Canada as we know it today.

How times have changed. Today, the Senate, also known as the Upper or Red Chamber, is the most controversial part of federal government.

Opening of 36th parliament in 1998 in the Senate

Few view it as the chamber of "sober second thought," as Sir John A. Macdonald called it. Instead, the Senate is regarded by many as undemocratic, needless, expensive, a gilt-edged retirement playpen, and Senate positions are seen as patronage plums with which the prime minister rewards party hacks, friends, and failed politicians. Everyone, it seems, wants the Senate reformed or abolished. In 1874, the third Governor General, Lord Dufferin, called the Senate "an absurdly effete body — nothing but a political infirmary and a bribery fund."

Despite current opposition, the Senate was created to ensure balanced representation for all regions of Canada regardless of population, in other words, to ensure the less populated provinces have some say in the nation's government. Ontario, Quebec, the four Western provinces together, and the three Maritime provinces together each have 24 senators. Newfoundland has six and the three territories each have one, yielding a total of 105. Senators are selected by the prime minister and appointed by the governor general. Once appointed, senators serve until they decide to resign or until they reach the ripe age of 75, whichever comes first.

Initially, there was a fear that if senators were elected, the Senate would challenge the authority of the House, leading to logjams and an unworkable government. All the Confederation-makers agreed that the Senate should be weak. Their solution was to appoint senators, rather than have them elected. In spite of considerable discussion over the years on how to reform the Senate, no significant changes have been made.

Normally there are 105 senators, although this number can vary. In 1990, for instance, Prime Minister Brian Mulroney temporarily raised the number of senators to 112 with help from a never-before-used clause in the British North America Act. His reason: to ensure that the bill introducing the controversial Goods and Services Tax would be passed.

In theory, the Senate has the same power as the House of Commons, except that it cannot introduce bills relating to finance or budgets. In practice, however, most bills are introduced in the House. To become law, all bills must be signed by both the Senate and House of Commons. Thus the Senate provides some protection against the majority party abusing power.

Senate Senility

Until 1965, when a retirement age was set at 75, Senate appointments were given for life. As a result, Canada is the only country in the world with the honour of having had members of parliament over 100 years old. David Work, a New Brunswick Conservative, spent 38 years as a Senator until his death in 1905 at age 102. George Dessaules, a Quebec Liberal, was a Senator for 23 years until his death in 1930 at age 102. During this long tenure Mr. Dessaules only made two short speeches.

Parliament & Politics: Steering The Ship of State

Fancy dress ball in the Senate in 1896   – City of Ottawa Archives, CA0190

The Senate meets only three afternoons a week, on Tuesdays, Wednesdays, and Thursdays. Because senators do not have the constant worry of getting re-elected, there is little of the posturing, grandstanding, and adversarial tactics that often characterize the House of Commons. Government business is not necessarily given priority in the Senate, there are no time limits on debates, and there is no Question Period, so senators have more time than MPs to introduce concerns that might be difficult to address in the House. The debates are restrained and speeches are generally short and to the point. As an eminent parliamentarian said, "It is a work-shop, not a theatre." The Senate, especially through its committees, performs much useful work in analyzing and amending bills.

The Independence of the House and Senate

The Canadian parliamentary system has been designed to include certain checks and balances so that too much power does not accumulate in one place. To that end, the Commons and Senate were designed to function independently. This independence has grown to the point where the two chambers are perhaps overly protective of their individual powers. One chamber never acknowledges even the existence of the other, instead referring to it as "the other place," or "another place." This divide, however, goes beyond simple verbal games. In addition to separate chambers, the House and Senate each have their own security staffs and offices, separate buses to ferry people about the parliamentary precinct, and separate environmental staff and janitors.

Committees

There are approximately 30 House, Senate and joint committees, each with 7 to 14 members. Their purpose is to study proposed legislation in detail and amend it as appropriate. Committees can call expert witnesses and are open to the public. Some of these committees are of such ongoing relevance that they have been made permanent and are called standing committees. Their membership can change from session to session.

Each committee has members from all parties represented in the House of Commons, in proportion to the number of party seats. The chairperson is elected by the committee from among government party members, except for two important committees, the Standing Committee on Public Accounts and the Standing Joint Committee on the Scrutiny of Regulations, where the chairpersons are selected from committee members representing the official opposition party. The Standing Committee on Procedure and House Affairs, which includes the party whips, recommends to the House which members should sit on the various committees. Committee membership can change from session to session.

Governor General

The governor general is the nominal head of state and representative of the Crown, that is, the Monarch of Great Britain and Canada. This position is mostly ceremonial and symbolic; the real power lies with the prime minister and the cabinet. The governor general's duties include representing the queen or king in Canada in various ceremonies, including opening new sessions of parliament. Of more significance, the governor general also has the right to discuss policy with the prime minister, to offer advice, and to help ensure that the nation continues to be governed accordingly.

The governor general signs all bills before they become law, calls on the leader of a party to form a government, and must give permission before an election can be called. He or she must remain neutral and not express political

> ## Some Interesting Governors General
>
> To date, the only female governors general have been Jeanne Sauvé, from 1984 to 1990 and Adrienne Clarkson, who was appointed in 1999.
>
> Lord Tweedsmuir created the Governor General Literary Awards in 1936; these are considered to be the most prestigious awards given for literary achievement in Canada. Canada's literati anxiously await the list of nominees each year.
>
> Governor General Lord Grey donated the ultimate prize in football, the Grey Cup, in 1909. The equivalent prize in hockey, the Stanley Cup, was donated by Governor General Lord Stanley in 1893.

Governor General Hnatyshyn with Queen Elizabeth — LIBRARY OF PARLIAMENT

opinions, nor become involved in party politics. The governor general plays an important role in the system of checks and balances that help stabilize our government, as he or she can, in exceptional circumstances, refuse to sign a bill or refuse to allow an election to be called.

The governor general is appointed by the prime minister for a term of usually five to seven years and retains the post even if the government changes. He or she is the official Commander in Chief of the armed forces and Chief Companion of the Order of Canada.

Since 1952 all governors general have been Canadian-born. Before this, they were selected from among the ranks of British aristocrats.

The governor general has two official residences: Rideau Hall located a few kilometres from the Hill (this is well worth a visit, especially for the New Year's levee, and the June garden party when the grounds are open to the public and you can meet the governor general), and La Citadelle in Québec City.

How Laws are Made

Bills that are passed into law fall into one of two categories, government or private members' bills. The large majority are government bills. Enacting government bills is the principal means for the ruling party to institute its policies. The first step in the long process of enacting a law is for the sponsoring department to present to cabinet the policy (not the bill) it would like enacted. This is examined, usually by a cabinet committee and, when approved, the Legislation Section of the Department of Justice prepares a draft bill, transforming the policy into legislative terms. It is then reviewed by cabinet committee and then approved by cabinet. Only then is the bill ready to go to parliament.

All bills involving financial matters must be introduced in the House of Commons. All other bills can be introduced in either the House of Commons or the Senate. A bill goes through three readings. The first is simply a formality that introduces the bill. A vote must be held at second and third readings, and every time an amendment is proposed during debate. Votes are also held on points of procedure during debates.

During the second reading, the policies and principles, but not specific details, of a bill are debated. If the bill passes, it is sent to a committee which analyzes it clause by clause and makes detailed amendments. In some cases, the committee may not report back to the House of Commons, so the bill dies; this is the fate of most private members' bills. A bill that involves taxation is dealt with by the entire House, in what is called a committee of the whole. In this case, the mace is hung under the Table to indicate a committee meeting is in progress rather than a formal sitting of the House. Once a bill is reported back to the House it is debated in what is known as the "report stage." The fine details are discussed and amendments may be proposed. Once a bill passes this stage, it is usually given third and final reading after only a short debate.

The bill is then sent to the Senate, where it goes through the same process of three readings. The Senate may pass the bill, defeat it (but not if it involves taxation or finance), or send it back to the House with amendments.

Because numerous votes are required, they are usually held by voice to save time, with each MP saying "yea" or "nay," and the Speaker deciding which has the majority. If there is doubt about the voice vote, five or more MPs can rise and demand a recorded vote. A recorded vote is a serious matter, for if a government bill is defeated, the government will usually, according to long-established tradition, resign or ask for a dissolution of the House. Buzzers sound throughout the Centre Block to summon MPs to the chamber. The Speaker requests all those in favour to stand. They nod to the Speaker one by one as the clerk calls out their name and records their vote. Votes usually follow party lines, but it can be an exciting time if the majority is small and some members are sick or absent.

A large part of the House's time is concentrated on financial legislation, especially on bills to authorize the spending of money, called "supply" bills, and bills to authorize the raising of revenue by taxation, called "ways and means" bills.

Any member who is not a minister may bring in a private member's bill, usually on subjects on which the government has not expressed a policy. Members are free to vote as they please and the government will not resign if the bill is defeated. Because these bills are of lower priority than government bills, most do not get beyond first reading. Nevertheless, they serve a useful purpose in drawing attention to situations that may need to be seriously considered.

Once bills have been passed by both the House of Commons and Senate, royal assent is given at a ceremony in the Senate, presided over by the governor general, or more often, a judge of the Supreme Court. This usually takes place at the end of the day's sitting and often includes several bills. As for the Throne Speech, the Gentleman Usher of the Black Rod goes to the House of Commons and knocks three times on the door to summon MPs, who then go to the Senate where they stand in front of the bar to watch the ceremony. The governor general then formally signs the bills.

You too can be heard in parliament. Any Canadian citizen may submit a petition to their MP. It must be signed by at least 25 people and should request specific action to be taken that lies within the jurisdiction of the House of Commons. All petitions are answered and may result in legislation. Between 5,000 and 9,000 petitions are presented to the House every session.

The Supreme Court in January 2000. First Row: F. Iacobucci, C. L'Heureux-Dubé, Chief Justice B.McLachlin, C.D.Gonthier, J.C.Major. Back Row: L.Arbour, M.Bastarache, W.I.C.Binnie, L.LeBel
– PHILLIPE LANDREVILLE INC./SUPREME COURT OF CANADA

Courts and Judges

An important cornerstone of Canadian government is that no one, not even the government itself, is above the law. A system of courts and judges has been established to ensure that the law does indeed have precedence — and independence.

The courts are arranged in a hierarchy, with a right of appeal progressing from the lower courts to those at higher levels. The Supreme Court sits at the top of the pyramid and in addition to being the court of last appeal, it also rules on the Constitution and the Charter of Rights and Freedoms. The Supreme Court is located a short distance from the Hill. In addition, there are provincial supreme courts, county and district courts, and minor provincial courts.

Although Supreme Court judges are appointed by cabinet, effectively until age 75, there is a clear division of power between the judiciary and government. Judges and the courts are completely independent of political influence.

The Media and Other Influences

In today's electronic world, the media plays a significant role in democratic government. Politics is hot news and people crave information about politicians and their activities, particularly anything of a scandalous nature. Reporting of events at parliament comes via: live television coverage of debates and question period; television coverage of special events and happenings; and reports by newspaper and radio.

By informing citizens, the media helps to ensure there is little secrecy, thus minimizing the possible abuse of power. The media has become so powerful it is known as the "Fourth Estate." It has become the eyes, ears, and conscience of the people. Because no cameras or tape recorders are allowed in the House, politicians often make policy announcements and important comments outside the chamber for the benefit of the media, in effect, speaking directly to the people rather than to their colleagues. A good place to watch these media scrums is from the House foyer and the corridor leading to the Rotunda where, often after question period, a mob of reporters thrust microphones and shout questions at cabinet ministers emerging from the chamber.

There are other groups who have an influence on government and help shape its outcomes, including lobbyists, poll-takers, and activists. These people share one characteristic, they are not elected, yet they still form a part of the voice of the people that the elected members of parliament must listen to.

President and Mrs. John Kennedy enter the House of Commons with
Prime Minister Diefenbaker in 1961
– National Archives of Canada, PA112430

The People
on the Hill

WITH a population of over 3,000, its imposing Gothic stone walls, and long-standing traditions, some dating back to the Middle Ages, the Hill seems like a fortified medieval town. But don't be fooled — the Hill incorporates the most modern technology and employs some of the brightest minds and most creative talents in the country. For each MP (301) and Senator (105) there are approximately eight additional people working behind the scenes to make the Hill run smoothly. They include lawyers, artists, clerks, security staff, pages, curators, printers, guides, janitors, librarians, chefs, secretaries, researchers, messengers, carpenters, carvers and many more. In this chapter we will look at some of the more interesting people who inhabit — and have inhabited — the Hill and who, through their skills and personalities, have made it the most special place in Canada.

Parliamentarians: Quirks and Incidents

Over the years, many interesting, even idiosyncratic, MPs and senators have strutted on the parliamentary stage, caught in the floodlight of never-ending media scrutiny.

Sir John A. Macdonald

Any compendium of colourful characters must start with Sir John A. Macdonald. Known as "Old Tomorrow" for his always-cautious approach, John A. cut an imposing figure with his blazing eyes, curly black hair, and whisky-veined nose. He had a sharp mind and was an effective, if not always eloquent, speaker.

Chapter 10

Macdonald was a strong leader, playing a key role in Canada's Confederation. He also developed a reputation for imbibing, a habit that was no doubt helped by the saloon below the House of Commons. For instance, the Toronto *Globe* described his condition during an all-night debate in April 1878: "To say that Sir John A. Macdonald was on Friday night somewhat under the influence of liquor would be a grossly inadequate representation of the fact. He was simply drunk, in the plain, ordinary sense of that word. As the night wore on, he became still more so ... and had to be hid away by his friends; if not in shame, at least in pity...."

Sir John was forced from office in the Pacific Scandal of 1873. During the 1872 election campaign he had accepted $300,000 from the Canadian Pacific Railway. Toward the end of the campaign, he sent a telegram to the owner of the CP railway requesting more money. "I must have another ten thousand.... Do not fail me. Answer today." Although Macdonald's Conservatives won the election, he was subsequently denied office when the telegram was made public.

Sir John A. Macdonald's funeral procession, 1891   – NATIONAL ARCHIVES OF CANADA, C7126

Louis Riel Makes an Entrance

Louis Riel was elected to Parliament in 1873 and 1874 as the Member for Provencher in Manitoba. As the charismatic leader of the Red River Rebellion, he was a wanted man and had the entire country searching for him. Nevertheless, one day he managed to enter the Centre Block by a side entrance accompanied by another MP. They approached the Clerk of the House who, not recognizing Riel, administered the oath and had Riel sign the roll. Only as Riel was leaving did the clerk notice the name on the roll and call the Minister of Justice. Riel never occupied his seat in the House and, in 1875, the House declared him an outlaw. He was hanged for treason in 1885.

Forgetful Arthur Meighen

Arthur Meighen, prime minister in the 1920s, was blessed with a formidable memory for facts and speeches. Unfortunately, this was countered to some degree by his legendary absentmindedness in managing his day-to-day affairs. One day, having forgotten his golf bag, he played an entire round of golf using only one club: a putter.

First Woman on the Hill

Agnes Macphail was born in Grey County, Ontario, in 1890. She entered politics to fight for farmers' rights and then took up the great battle to secure increased rights for women. In 1920, the first time women were allowed to vote and run in a federal election, Macphail was the only woman elected and served until 1940. In 1943 she was elected as one of the first two women to Ontario's provincial legislature.

Seats, Seats Everywhere but ...

In 1925, Charles Macdonald won the riding of Prince Albert, Saskatchewan, as a member of the Liberal party. Before he could sit for the first time in the House, he was asked to give up his seat to William Lyon Mackenzie

The People on the Hill

King, who promised to reward Macdonald with a Senate appointment. But time dragged on, and it was 1935 before King kept his promise. Due to ill health, Macdonald was unable to attend a single session of the Senate. Macdonald now has the sad record of being the only person ever to have gained both a seat in the House and Senate, but never sat in either.

Women are Persons

Cairine Wilson, born in Montreal in 1885, was appointed Canada's first woman senator in 1930. The appointment did not come easily, however, as it required that the Privy Council in Great Britain overturn a ruling by the Supreme Court of Canada that stated women were not "persons," and therefore could not be appointed to public office. The court case marked a milestone for women in Canada.

Sharp-Shooting Speaker

George Black, Speaker from 1930 to 1935, was undoubtedly the most colourful character ever to sit in the House's grand chair. He mushed his way over the Klondike gold trail of 1898, panned for gold, and made a fortune — only to lose it. He fought and was wounded in World War I. On his return from overseas, he was re-elected to the House three times as a Yukon representative. During his tenure as Speaker, he kept a loaded pistol in his chambers and would shoot rabbits from the window when he saw them nibbling on the nearby shrubbery. One day, after bagging six hares, Black called in reporters to announce his exploit. In 1935, suffering health problems, he stepped down as Speaker and MP. During his recuperation, his wife won his seat, becoming only the second woman to sit in the House. By 1940, Black was fully recovered and his wife stood aside allowing him his seat again. He left the House in 1949, at age 78.

Job Security?

If you think you have problems with job security, then you should have pity for poor Lloyd Francis. He first contested his Ottawa riding in 1962, and lost. The following year he tried again, and won. He was defeated in 1965; elected in 1968; defeated in 1972; elected in 1974; defeated in 1979; elected in 1980; and was defeated for the final time in 1984. In all, he contested nine elections and, like a metronome, regularly alternated between the euphoria of victory (4 times) and the crush of defeat (5 times). Although he lost one more election than he won, he spent all but five years in Parliament between 1963 and 1984.

The Eccentric
William Lyon Mackenzie King

Prime Minister W.L.M. King leaving
Laurier House, 1930
– National Archives of Canada, C9059

Despite having been the country's longest-serving prime minister, William Lyon Mackenzie King was one of the most eccentric, least-liked, and least understood leaders in Canadian history. King kept the most irregular hours often choosing to work at home rather than on the Hill. He was merciless with his staff, who had to cater to his every whim. He was also a confirmed bachelor who built Kingsmere estate in the Gatineau hills, which he bequeathed to the nation. The fake castle ruins he had constructed there fit wonderfully into the landscape giving it a look which very much appears like a Scottish highland.

General DeGaulle with Prime Minister W.L.M. King in 1944
– National Archives of Canada, C47572

The People on the Hill

During the War he sent a secret cipher under priority "Most Immediate" to Canada's High Commission in London. On decoding the message, the staff were dumbfounded to discover that King was requesting that some of the stones from England's parliament, which had just been struck by German bombs, be retrieved and sent to Canada so he could incorporate them into his "ruins" at Kingsmere.

King's fascination for occult and psychic experiences was perhaps a replacement for the lack of close friends and the loneliness of high office. He often sat in séances that involved "table-rapping" and spoke with his late mother and deceased relatives and colleagues. He also recorded and interpreted his dreams, referring to them as "visions." Although aware of Freud's theories, King's interpretations were simpler and more pragmatic, generally providing confirmation for his actions or urging him to be more conscientious in his work.

Churchill Exhorts

One of Sir Winston Churchill's most famous speeches was made in the chamber of the House of Commons on New Year's eve, 1941. Although the war had turned in the Allies' favour, he gave a rousing speech to ensure ongoing Canadian commitment to the war effort. He described

Sir Winston Churchill addresses the House of Commons, 1941
– NATIONAL ARCHIVES OF CANADA, C22140

how the French nation had been defeated, and how prior to invasion he had warned French generals Britain would fight on alone, whatever happened with France. The generals told the French prime minister that, "In three weeks England will have her neck wrung like a chicken." Churchill continued, "Some chicken! Some neck!" a phrase that was to become one of his most famous and most inspirational battle cries.

Diefenbaker the Orator

John Diefenbaker, prime minister from 1957 to 1963, was an orator of considerable repute. He seldom stuck to his written text but played the audience like an experienced fly fisherman works a familiar trout stream for a nibble. The "Chief" did not believe in making logical, structured arguments; instead, he counted on emotional impact. "It's a long road that has no ash cans," he once exclaimed to a rather bewildered audience. Yogi Berra would be proud.

Once launched, Diefenbaker would throw his body and soul into every delivery, his voice ranging from *basso profundo* to a high-pitched falsetto, with occasional horse-like whinnies and other interjections. As described by acclaimed journalist Charles Lynch, "He would point the avenging finger, and he would flap his arms like a pelican venting its wings prior to takeoff. The eyes would burn and the tightly waved hair

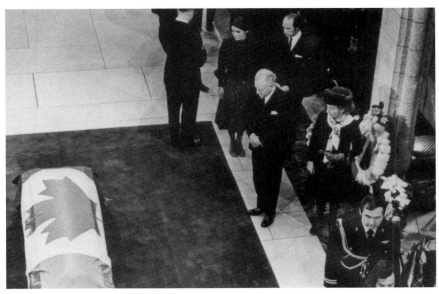

Lester Pearson lies in state with Prime Minister Pierre Trudeau, Mrs. Margaret Trudeau, Governor General Roland Michener and Mrs. Michener in attendance.
– National Archives of Canada, PA121708

The People on the Hill

113

would fly and, at the height of his powers, the crowds would roar and people would clutch at his garments."

Diefenbaker idolized Sir John A. Macdonald and had a collection of Macdonald memorabilia, including a mantel clock which had to be carried to whichever of the three parliamentary offices Diefenbaker was working in that day. Every January 11th, the Chief would lead an entourage of Tory MPs to Macdonald's statue and lay a wreath to commemorate the birthday of the Father of Confederation. The Chief was a very vain man, and it was said that his happiest moment came when a party candidate introduced him by saying that Macdonald and Diefenbaker were the two greatest Conservatives ever.

The Formidable Trudeau

Pierre Elliott Trudeau was admired by everyone for his intellect, which resembled a computer in its capacity for memory and linear, cogent analysis. He devoted intense concentration to all his tasks and often knew more about the issues under discussion at the cabinet table than the responsible ministers. His interests were eclectic and his knowledge monumental. In argument, he would use his prodigious memory and elegant, almost sneering style to destroy both the argument, and confidence, of his opponents.

Elegant and Formidable

Born in Prud'homme, Saskatchewan, in 1922, Jeanne Sauvé went on to establish a brilliant career, first as a journalist and broadcaster, then as a politician. She was initially elected to federal parliament in 1972 and soon became a member of cabinet. In 1980, she became the first woman Speaker of the House. In 1984, she became Canada's first woman governor general, a position she held until 1990.

Canada's First Woman Prime Minister

Kim Campbell was born in Port Alberni, British Columbia, in 1947. She studied political science before turning to law and then politics. She won a seat in the British Columbia legislature in 1986 and then won a federal seat in 1988. She held various cabinet positions before becoming leader of the Progressive Conservative party. She served as the first, and to date, only woman prime minister. Her tenure lasted from June to November, 1993, when the Conservative party fell to a disastrous defeat in which the party garnered only two seats in the House of Commons. In 1996 she was appointed as Canadian Consul General in Los Angeles.

Pages

Both the House of Commons and the Senate employ pages during sessions. They carry messages, bring glasses of water, distribute documents, and generally facilitate the operation of the chambers as well as helping the members remain in touch with each other and their offices. There are 42 pages in the House with about a dozen on duty at any given time. Both male and female pages are hired, all bilingual first-year university students. In the old days, they had to be male and shorter than 5 feet 6 inches so they would not obscure MPs' views in the chamber — or make the MPs look any less grand.

In the nineteenth century, page boys would hold impromptu parliaments during dinner recesses. A "Speaker" was selected who would then don the Speaker's gown and sit in the chair while the rest took up positions in the government and opposition benches. Many members took an interest in the pages' parliament and even Sir John Macdonald occasionally gave debating pointers to the young aspirants.

Pages distributing documents   – Library of Parliament

The People on the Hill

Gordon Slater: The Voice of the Peace Tower

Gordon Slater is a musician of extraordinary and varied talent. In addition to pounding the Carillon keyboard as the Dominion Carillonneur for over two decades, he also plays the bassoon and contrabassoon for the Ottawa Symphony Orchestra, conducts a sixty-piece amateur orchestra, and leads a baroque trio from the harpsichord. Long before he received formal musical training at the Toronto Conservatory of Music and the University of Toronto, he learned to play the carillon from his father, also an accomplished carillonneur. "It's an unusual job, but a real honour to control the voice of the Peace Tower. I try to make the voice speak with integrity and clarity."

Carvers of Stone and Wood

One of the most delightful features on the Hill is the hundreds of delightful stone carvings that can be found in various nooks and corners. The carvings include an amazing range of gargoyles, animals, grotesques, and likenesses of politicians as well as some of the carvers themselves.

Some of the notables whose stone images grace the Hill include about 20 prime ministers, King George V, King Edward VII, Senator Charles Bishop, journalist Grattan O'Leary, Premier Orlando of Italy, and many

Grotesque near entrance to the Centre Block — HANS TAMMEMAGI

Maurice Joanisse: Portrait of a Sculptor

Maurice Joanisse has been carving stone on Parliament Hill for three decades and still exudes enthusiasm when he speaks about his labour of love. His father, a tombstone craftsman, taught him to work with stone from an early age. Joining the parliamentary stone carving group in 1971 as an apprentice, he learned the intricacies of Gothic and Romanesque carving under the tutelage of Eleanor Milne. Since then he has been involved in creating about a hundred original carvings. One of his favourites is the series of ten panels depicting prehistoric life in Canada. These panels grace the House of Commons above the north and south galleries. Although the number of stone carvers has diminished from a peak of 14 in the early part of this century, to only Joanisse today, the work continues unabated. A series of ten busts of famous railroad builders is planned for the Hall of Honour in front of the Railway Room.

117

more. It is, however, no longer acceptable to make a carving of a living person; it is customary that the individual be dead for at least 50 years before immortalization in stone.

Today, the grotesques and gargoyles are among the Hill's most popular features, despite the fact that their "frightful" appearances caused great controversy when first introduced.

Although some stone carvings were done for the original Centre Block, it was not until the construction of the new Centre Block, with the encouragement of architect John Pearson, that carving became a major decorative form. The first sculptor was Walter Allan, who worked with a team of carvers. Ira Lake, an American sculptor, was hired in 1926 to carve the interior of the Memorial Chamber. Cleophas Soucy became Dominion Sculptor in 1948, after he had been working at the Hill for over a decade in a part-time capacity. He worked with an assistant, Coeur-de-Lion MacCarthy, and a team of thirteen carvers. They completed the carving of the Senate chamber and the large lion and unicorn at the entrance to the Peace Tower. In 1950, William Oosterhoff became the official sculptor. He was responsible for the frieze around the ceiling of the Commons chamber which depicts the floral emblems and leading industries of the provinces.

Eleanor Milne, a gifted designer and drawer as well as carver, became the next official sculptor in 1962. Born in St. John, New Brunswick, in 1925, her interests include carving in stone, wood and bronze, stained glass window design, and water-colour painting. She and her team carved the ten-panel "History of Canada" frieze around the gallery of the Commons foyer. She also designed and supervised the construction of twelve stained glass windows in the Commons chamber. She has carved numerous other works which are found on the Hill as well as at St. Andrews Church, Ottawa, and the Yukon and Northwest Territories legislatures.

In many cases Milne's work was done on location, using scaffolds and working at night so the noise and dust did not interfere with the workings of government. Today, the carving is done in a workshop on Somerset Street and the finished product trucked to the hill and inserted into place. In 1993, Maurice Joanisse succeeded Milne as Dominion Sculptor.

The fine stone carvings on the Hill are complemented by many beautiful wood carvings, particularly in the House of Commons and Senate chambers and in the Library. Unfortunately, the names of the carvers are not known as the wood carving was generally contracted to different carpentry companies and the names of the specific artisans were not recorded. A wood carver is presently employed by the House of Commons carpentry shop; he created the beaver on the altar of the Sean O'Sullivan Chapel in East Block.

Detail of wood carvings in the Library

– JANET BROOKS

Interior Decorators

The House of Commons has its own interior designer who assists MPs in decorating their offices. MPs may decorate after each election, and cabinet ministers are allowed more expensive furnishings. Interior decorating is a big operation and requires many skills and much craftsmanship. For this reason, a carpenter is on the full-time payroll. Interior decorators are conservation minded and considerable work is done to recycle as much furniture as possible.

Wrought Iron

An important part of decoration in Gothic architecture is formed by wrought iron. On the Hill good examples are found at the top of the wall along Wellington Street and the filigree on the roof of East Block. Paul Beau of Montreal handcrafted many fine pieces between 1919 and 1926, including fenders and fire irons for ministers' fireplaces, the House of Commons seal, inkstand, and the calendar that rests on The Table in the House of Commons.

Wrought-iron calendar in the House of Commons

– ANDY SHOTT

Executive Chef Judson Simpson

– ANDY SHOTT

Not only do armies march on their stomachs, but so do parliamentarians — and Canadian parliamentarians get to do so in sumptuous surroundings where they enjoy mouth-watering gourmet cuisine. Chef Judson Simpson is the man responsible for making the sixth-floor restaurant in the Centre Block one of the finest eating establishments in the world. "Food is universal," Chef Simpson explains, "it is always involved in meetings and acts as a buffer, a comfort zone that brings MPs together, even if they are adversaries in the House."

The greatest challenge Chef Simpson faces is to satisfy the wide variety of tastes, as MPs and senators come from all walks of life and from all parts of this country, and sometimes from other countries too; he must also feed foreign dignitaries, who often have bizarre requests. His most unusual meal featured either emu or ostrich for almost every course. The dessert was a meringue made from the white of an ostrich egg — fifteen times the size of a chicken egg. Simpson is proud to be Canadian and has demonstrated that our chefs are some of the best in the world. In 1988, he captained a Canadian team to the grand gold medal at the World Culinary Olympics in Germany; in 1992 he led a team to the silver prize.

The parliamentary dining room   – ANDY SHOTT

The People on the Hill

Tour Guides

About 30 to 40 guides are employed during summer, less during winter; they are university students selected from across Canada and must be bilingual.

Security and Bombs

The sergeant-at-arms is head of security for the House of Commons and the House of Commons part of the parliamentary precinct, which includes Langevin Block and other nearby buildings. For ceremonial duties, he wears a black uniform and a cocked hat. He has a staff of over 200 to help him keep order. Video cameras, walkie-talkies, and panic buttons in some of the parliamentarians' desks form part of their equipment. The House of Commons security command centre is in the Wellington building. The Senate has a totally independent security staff with its headquarters in the Victoria building.

We are fortunate that political acts of violence are not common in Canada. However, there have been exceptions. For example, in May 18, 1966, an explosion was heard in the mens' washroom outside the House of Commons. Question period continued unabated, but shortly afterwards Prime Minister Lester Pearson was handed a note stating that a man had just killed himself with an explosive. Paul Joseph Chartier had been sitting in the gallery with five sticks of dynamite under his coat and, seeking to arm the device, had gone into the washroom where he apparently mistimed the fuse. A note found in his pocket read, "Mr. Speaker, Gentlemen, I might as well give you a blast to wake you up. For one whole year I have thought of nothing but how to exterminate as many of you as possible. The only bills you pass are the ones that line your pockets. I move that we elect a president right now. All in favour, raise your right hand. If not in favour, God help you." A serious tragedy was averted only due to Dame Fortune, for who knows how many would have died if he had thrown the dynamite onto the front benches of the House. As it was, the House adjourned for an hour and then reconvened as though nothing had happened.

Hansard

Hansard is the written record of all debates and of question period in the House of Commons and the Senate. It is named after R.C. Hansard who printed the debates from the British House of Commons from 1812 to 1892. Until about 1990, debates were recorded by teams of shorthand reporters who sat in the chamber, but now the speeches are tape recorded.

Two Hansard monitors note interruptions and other disturbances. The tapes are typed into a word processor and edited to remove ums, ahs, snores, and other items which do not contribute to the discussion, but heckling, name calling, and other interruptions are included. The edited transcript is printed and sent for review by the MPs who spoke. They have three hours to make corrections but are not allowed to alter the meaning or sense of what they originally said. The text is then translated into the other official language and is electronically printed at the Queen's Printer overnight. This entire process is carried out so efficiently and by such skilled people that by 9:00 next morning, the Hansard of the previous day's debate is on each MP's desk.

You may enjoy looking up Hansard at your public library and reading the speeches that your local MP has given to see what stance he/she has taken on controversial issues.

The Press

The media is an integral part of today's "wired world" and bringing the events on the Hill into our living rooms is big business. The Parliamentary Press Gallery has almost 400 full-time members and over 2,000 part-time members. Some of the television reporters and newspaper columnists themselves — the people behind the microphones — become national icons, such as Mike Duffy, Charles Lynch, and Knowlton Nash. The National Press Building is located at 150 Wellington Street, across the street from the Hill.

Changing of the Guard

every summer morning. Kids and adults alike will be thrilled at the sight of soldiers, resplendent in old-fashioned scarlet tunics and tall bearskin hats, bearing rifles while marching and wheeling with great precision. The Guard is composed of student reservists from the Governor-General's Foot Guards and the Canadian Grenadier Guards. Starting at 9:30 a.m., the Guard marches to the Hill from nearby Cartier Square Drill Hall and moves along Laurier, Elgin and Wellington Streets accompanied by a regimental band.

Sound and Light Show

Canadian history comes alive in this dramatic show where lights and images are projected on the majestic Parliament Buildings accompanied by inspiring music. For 30 minutes you will be entertained and informed. Both French and English shows run from mid May to early September. Show times and the number of daily shows vary during the season, so call in advance.

Canada Day

On this special day, over one hundred thousand people, including the governor general and prime minister, fill the grounds of the Hill and surrounding area to watch an extravagant performance showcasing talent from across the country. Streets near the Hill are closed to traffic and are crammed with celebrants bedecked with Canadian flags and red and white hats and tattoos; buskers entertain everywhere. The day is topped off with a spectacular fireworks show.

New Year's Eve

On New Year's Eve, upwards of 30,000 visitors crowd the Hill to welcome in the new year with good cheer and lively entertainment, including on-stage performances, a carillon concert, and a fine display of fireworks at the stroke of midnight.

Winterlude

Celebrated for ten days in mid-February, Winterlude is one of the top winter festivals in North America. Although most of the celebrations take place elsewhere, the Hill hosts a fascinating ice sculpture display where representatives from each province and territory turn an ice block, the size of a small house, into a piece of art that represents their region. It's fun to watch the axes, picks, hand and motor saws sending ice chips in all directions.

Ice sculpture during Winterlude — Hans Tammemagi

Explore on Your Own

If you have an independent spirit, or simply wish to amble at your leisure, it's easy to conduct your own tour. The Memorial Chamber and observation deck in the Peace Tower, and Confederation Hall in the Centre Block, can be visited without the need for a formal tour; directions can be obtained at the Visitors' Centre in the Centre Block or at the InfoTent north of West Block (summer only).

A class visits parliament, 1938 — CITY OF OTTAWA ARCHIVES, CA0190

A stroll around the Hill is always rewarding. Statues and other points of interest, such as the summer pavilion and the cat sanctuary, are described in Chapter 8.

The artwork on the Hill is both impressive and unique. The number of stone carvings is unsurpassed in any set of buildings in North America. But there is much more, including wood carvings, stained glass windows, wrought iron, and paintings. A tour of this artisanship is very worthwhile. Here is a list of some of the artworks you may wish to visit on your personal tour:

Inside Centre Block

- 12 stained glass windows in the House of Commons displaying the provincial and territorial flowers
- a stone frieze in the foyer of the House of Commons
- paintings of prime ministers in the Commons foyer, paintings along the corridor to the Rotunda depicting vivid scenes from Canadian history
- large paintings of First World War scenes in the Senate
- stone busts of former stone carvers in the Senate foyer
- paintings of British kings and queens in the Senate foyer. Look for Queen Victoria's portrait that was twice saved from flames. Does she have one shrunken arm?
- wood carvings of flowers, masks and mythical creatures in the Library
- wonderful stone carving and stained glass in the Memorial Chamber

Stone carving and stained glass in the Memorial Chamber — HANS TAMMEMAGI

Outside

- a stone lion and unicorn flanking the main entrance to Centre Block; also note the smaller grotesques on the side of the Peace Tower
- four large gargoyles on the Peace Tower just below the clock face; they were designed as spouts for rain water
- busts of Thomas Fuller and John Pearson, the architects of the first and second Centre Blocks, respectively, stare out from the main walls on either side of the Peace Tower
- gargoyle in the likeness of Edgar Rhodes, past Speaker of the House (and MP for Cumberland, Nova Scotia). During construction of the new Centre Block, many of his suggestions were incorporated into the new edifice, such as the separate Speaker's entrance at the west side of the building. Outside the door, the stone sculptors, prohibited by tradition from carving lifelike images of real people, instead chiseled a gargoyle in Rhodes's likeness, complete with large nose and pince-nez glasses
- wrought-iron door handles by Paul Beau on the main door into the Centre Block and wrought iron on the fence along Wellington Street

Be sure to walk behind the Centre Block. Here you'll be rewarded with sweeping views of the rolling Gatineau hills. If you happen to be in Ottawa in fall, the soft, hazy undulating greens will be splashed with yellows and reds and burnished gold. Far below you will also see the Chaudière rapids; perhaps the breeze will even carry the muted sound of swirling, roaring water to the cliff top. If you are in a pensive mood, you

Stone and wrought-iron fence along Wellington Street   – Hans Tammemagi

Activities on the Hill

Wrought-iron caught on a red sky   – NCC/CCN

might imagine the days when logs by the thousands tumbled and clattered down wooden chutes to be assembled into giant rafts destined for the sawmills of Montreal.

As the sun sinks lower in the western sky and the light turns golden yellow, perhaps you'll pause and rest on a slab of granite below one of the many stalwart bronze figures. The playing light will highlight the different hues of yellows and browns in the sandstone blocks of the Library, softening and enriching the dramatic buttresses and ramparts. Peeking out from behind the roof of the Library, the Peace Tower will be bathed in bronze skylight and above it, the red and white of the flag will flap lazily in the breeze.

If you lean against the sun-warmed rock and close your eyes, you might hear the gentle murmur of voices in the breeze. If you listen carefully, you may be able to make out what these bronze statues — these men and women who worked to mould their vision of this nation — are saying. You will hear the voices of the past, the threads that formed the fabric of Canada.

As the chill of twilight descends, you'll emerge from this special place and turn your thoughts and footsteps homeward. But the next time you return, these ancient Gothic buildings will again be bathed in golden light and you'll be ready, again, to explore the Hill.

The original Centre Block under construction, circa 1865
– NATIONAL PHOTOGRAPHY COLLECTION C-3039

Further Reading

Anon., *The Federal Legislative Process in Canada*, Minister of Supply and Services, Ottawa, 1987.

Baird, David M., *Guide to the Geology and Scenery of the National Capital Area*, Geological Survey of Canada, Misc. Report 15, Ottawa, 1968.

Binks, K., *Library of Parliament Canada*, KCB Publications, Ottawa, 1979.

Bosco, Mark, *The Broadview Book of Canadian Parliamentary Anecdotes*, Broadview Press, Peterborough, 1988.

Bourrie, Mark, *Canada's Parliament Buildings*, Hounslow Press, Toronto, 1996.

Brado, Edward, *Brado's Guide to Ottawa*, Quarry Press, Kingston, 1991.

Brault, L., and D. Lett, *Parliament Hill*, National Capital Commission, Ottawa, no date.

Brault, Lucien, *The Mile of History*, National Capital Commission, Ottawa, 1981.

Davies, Blodwen, *Ottawa, Portrait of a Capital*, McGraw-Hill, 1954.

Dawson, R. MacGregor, W. F. Dawson, and N. Ward, *Democratic Government in Canada*, Fifth Edition, University of Toronto Press, Toronto, 1989.

Duhaime, Lloyd, *Hear! Hear! 125 years of debate in Canada's House of Commons*, Stoddart Publishing, Toronto, 1992.

Eggleston, Wilfrid, *The Queen's Choice — A Story of Canada's Capital*, National Capital Commission, Ottawa, 1961.

Forsey, Eugene A., *How Canadians Govern Themselves*, Library of Parliament, Ottawa, 1997.

Holzman, J., and R. Tosh, *Ottawa: Then and Now, Visitor's Guide*, Magic Light Publishing, Ottawa, 2000.

Hoy, Claire, *Nice Work: The Continuing Scandal of Canada's Senate*, McClelland & Stewart Inc., Toronto, 1999.

Levy, Gary, *Speakers of the Canadian House of Commons*, Library of Parliament, Ottawa, 1996.

Lund, Chris, *Stones of History; Canada's Houses of Parliament*, National Film Board and Malak, 1967.

Martin, Carol, and Kevin Burns (editors), *Ottawa, A Colour Guide*, Formac Publishing Company Limited, Halifax, 1997.

Merritt, Allen, S., and George W. Brown, *Canadians and their Government*, Fitzhenry & Whiteside, 1983.

Minton, Eric, *Ottawa: Reflections of the Past*, Nelson Foster and Scott, Toronto, 1974.

Phillips, R. A. J., *The East Block of the Parliament Buildings of Canada*, Queens Printer, Ottawa, 1967.

Riendeau, Roger, *A Brief History of Canada*, Fitzhenry & Whiteside, Markham, 2000

Robertson, Heather, *On the Hill; A People's Guide to Canada's Parliament*, McClelland & Stewart Inc., Toronto, 1992.

Young, Carolyn A., *The Glory of Ottawa: Canada's First Parliament Buildings*, McGill-Queens University Press, Montreal & Kingston, 1995.

Acknowledgements

I cannot begin to express the enormous pleasure writing *Exploring the Hill* has brought me; it has been a thrill and an honour to walk the grounds of the Hill, to explore the nooks and crannies of these wonderful Gothic buildings, and to meet the many talented and friendly people who work there.

None of this would have happened without the assistance of many people and organizations. I would like to thank everyone involved, and especially: Mr. Gilbert Parent, Speaker of the House of Commons for allowing access to the Hill; Gilles Brasseur, Public Works & Government Services Canada, who, unsuspectingly, drew me into this adventure when he hired me to perform an environmental audit of the Parliament Buildings; Tina Tsallas, Great Titles Incorporated, who found a publisher for this book; Kirk Hansen for providing a detailed and thoughtful review of the initial draft; and Richard Dionne, Fitzhenry & Whiteside, who did an excellent job of editing and improving the final draft. In particular, I am grateful to my wife, Allyson, for her unstinting support.

Much of the impact of this book comes from the photographs and figures it contains. I would like to thank the following for granting me permission to use their photographs: Andy Shott, Photographer for the House of Commons; Janet Brooks, Ottawa, an excellent photographer with a sensitive eye; the National Capital Commission; the Library of Parliament; the National Archives of Canada; the City of Ottawa Archives; Michael Bedford, Ottawa; and the Supreme Court of Canada.

Former Speaker Gilbert Parent standing in front of the Speaker's chair.   – ANDY SHOTT

Index

Index

Index

Index